Critical Issues in Educational Leadership Series
Joseph Murphy, Series Editor

Developing Educational Leaders: A Working Model:
The Learning Community in Action
CYNTHIA J. NORRIS, BRUCE G. BARNETT,
MARGARET R. BASOM, AND DIANE M. YERKES

Understanding and Assessing the Charter School Movement
JOSEPH MURPHY AND CATHERINE DUNN SHIFFMAN

School Choice in Urban America:
Magnet Schools and the Pursuit of Equity
CLAIRE SMREKAR AND ELLEN GOLDRING

Lessons from High-Performing Hispanic Schools:
Creating Learning Communities
PEDRO REYES, JAY D. SCRIBNER, AND
ALICIA PAREDES SCRIBNER, EDS.

Schools for Sale:Why Free Market Policies
Won't Improve America's Schools, and What Will
ERNEST R. HOUSE

Reclaiming Educational Administration as a Caring Profession
LYNN G. BECK

Cognitive Perspectives on Educational Leadership
PHILIP HALLINGER, KENNETH LEITHWOOD, AND
JOSEPH MURPHY, EDS.

Developing Educational Leaders

A WORKING MODEL: THE LEARNING COMMUNITY IN ACTION

Cynthia J. Norris
Bruce G. Barnett
Margaret R. Basom
Diane M. Yerkes

FOREWORD BY LINDA LAMBERT

Teachers College, Columbia University
New York and London

Published by Teachers College Press, 1234 Amsterdam Avenue, New York, NY 10027

Portions of Chapter 1 and the student journal excerpts in Chapter 2 are from "The Cohort: A Vehicle for Building Transformational Leadership Skills," by C. Norris, B. Barnett, M. Basom, and D. Yerkes, 1996, *Planning and Changing, 27*(3/4), pp. 145–164.

Library of Congress Cataloging-in-Publication Data

Developing educational leaders : a working model, the learning community in action / Cynthia J. Norris . . . [et al.].
    p. cm. — (Critical issues in educational leadership series)
    Includes bibliographical references (p.   ) and index.
    ISBN 0-8077-4184-1 (cloth) — ISBN 0-8077-4183-3 (pbk.)
    1. Educational leadership—United States.   2. School administrators—Training of—United States.   3. Community education—United States.   I. Norris, Cynthia J.   II. Series.

LB2805 .D46   2002
371.2'00973—dc21   2001053437

ISBN 0-8077-4183-3 (paper)
ISBN 0-8077-4184-1 (cloth)

Printed on acid-free paper
Manufactured in the United States of America

09 08 07 06 05 04 03 02   8 7 6 5 4 3 2 1

Contents

Foreword *by Linda Lambert*   vii

Introduction   1

1. The Learning Community   9

     Belief Statements and Assumptions   10
     The Need for Learning Communities   11
     Personal Empowerment Through Learning Communities   12
     Learning Communities Conceptualized   13
     Sociological and Psychological Nature of Groups   14
     Review of the Study   15
     Group Development: The Sociological Perspective   16
     Individual Development: The Psychological Perspective   19
     A Learning Community Model   24
     Implications for School Leadership   25
     Looking Ahead   30

2. Leadership and Community Development Through
Values Consciousness   31

     Values and Leadership   31
     Values Development   34
     Values and Ethics   36
     Values and Leadership Development   37
     Pathways of Values and Leadership Development   38
     Cycles of Growth   40
     Phases of Consciousness   41
     Summary   46
     Looking Ahead   46

3. Principals as Developing Leaders   48

     Students' Experience in Administrator Preparation Programs   50
     The Leaders   50

Overall Perspectives 72
Summary 74

4. Transformational Leadership: Conceptualized and Developed 75

Moral Leadership Through Care 75
Ethic of Care 78
Servant Leadership 80
Framing Leadership Perspectives 82
Leadership Perspective, Past and Present 83
Ethical Responsibilities of Transformational Leadership 85
The Need for Transformational Leaders 87
A Challenge to Those Who Prepare Leaders 88

5. Shaping the Curriculum to Foster Leadership Development
   Within Learning Communities 91

Content Curriculum 92
Process Curriculum 96
Role of the Professor 100
Instructional Methods 102
Summary 108

6. The Legacy of Learning Communities: Transfer to
   the Workplace 110

The Concept of Learning Transfer 111
Factors Affecting Transfer and Change 112
Transfer and Learning Communities 116
Final Thoughts on Transfer 125
Conclusion 126

Epilogue: The Impact of Our Work, Individually and Collectively 129

References 139

Index 149

About the Authors 158

Foreword

PREPARATION PROGRAMS for educational leaders are under siege. Charges of irrelevancy, failure to achieve administrative standards, and unprepared leaders are nationally pervasive. The charge that is the most resounding, yet not far from the truth, is that the universities have failed to educate enough leaders who can design and lead schools that will enable all children to be successful. The yawning achievement gap is laid at the feet of today's principals—and therefore those who prepared them.

Questionable preparation approaches are now accompanied by new options on the part of the participants. These potential leaders are beginning to avoid that nearly impossible job called the "principalship." Recognizing that the expectations and the stresses of the job are resulting in fewer qualified candidates, one cannot but wonder if part of this avoidance arises when they experience themselves as being unprepared to undertake such work. The effect is compounded: a startling lack of highly qualified educational leaders.

Bearing the burden of perceived school failure is a weighty one indeed. Such a burden can stimulate hopelessness, and it can stimulate change. Some of those changes have led to the "quick fix"—the new checklist, the new examination, faster delivery of technical content. Some states are looking for new vendors, including districts, regional academies, professional organizations, and a host of private entrepreneurs. Are we glimpsing the end of university preparation of educational leaders as we know it? I hope so.

We are yearning for another way. The authors of this book powerfully project new images of preparation onto the leadership landscape. These images sketch an ecological dynamic of interdependent and interlocking dimensions—"leadership development portrayed as a reciprocal process where a community of learners inspires both individual and group development."

Through ten years of research as a team of university professors from different parts of the country, Norris, Barnett, Basom, and Yerkes have discovered and designed a transformative approach involving recurring nested learning communities: a learning community of authors, of program participants, and of school staffs. The authors take us into the schools to witness the unfolding of communities of practice by those who experienced such communities in their university cohorts. Personal transformation leads to group transformation to school transformation.

You may well ask, Is transformation really possible? Ever since Siddhartha stepped foot outside his father's palace to find himself by the river as the Buddha, humankind has sought transformation. Are there things we know now that we only sought or imagined before? I propose that there are.

The authors have crafted assumptions and models evolved from practice and borrowed from deep and sustained study of the human journey. They assume that knowledge of self and others, an ethic of care, and a willingness to "share power through collective contribution" are "the foundation of community." A knowledge base regarding educational leadership—and now expressed in standards—is grist for the mill as participants construct knowledge and meaning together. This dance of content and process is constructivist in nature.

The model for preparation offered here suggests that through purpose, interaction, and interdependence within community, participants move through stages of development. These stages are expressed through evolving self-empowerment that leads to the empowerment of others and the community. When participants find themselves, and their values, situated in learning communities, they begin to see themselves in "the other."

From others, participants draw renewed strength in their own identities and confidence in their abilities to reform the world around them. Their capacities to care are unleashed. Thus emancipated, they become more inclusive, receptive, and global in their perspectives. By retaining a habit of reflection and self-understanding, together with continuing conversations, these commitments become actualized in schools. If participants transform who they are and how they think, the schools that they help create are different as well—different in a way that expresses deeply held values about the learning of all children.

I can bear witness to the claim that constructivist learning communities can be transformative. I have found it to be so. I wish I had read this book a decade ago, but no such gift was forthcoming before now. It has been a struggle, sometimes finding the right combinations of dialogue, reflection, content, and community—and sometimes missing the mark. These authors have brought their learning together in a way that is persuasive, understandable, and transferable.

As I ponder this profound work, two quotes seem apt: John Archibald Wheeler's words, "To my mind there must be, at the bottom of it all, not an equation, but an utterly simple idea. And to me that idea, when we finally discover it, will be so compelling, so inevitable, that we will say to one another, 'Oh, how beautiful. How could it have been otherwise?'", and Fritjof Capra's, "The main challenge of our time is to create and nurture sustainable communities."

I still believe that there is no better place in which to prepare leaders than the university, in partnership with districts and other agencies. However, if universities are to retain that central role, we must turn to the lessons in this remarkable book. Those of us engaged in educational preparation must take heed. We must not be satisfied with leadership preparation as it exists today.

—Linda Lambert

Introduction

EDUCATIONAL LEADERS increasingly are encouraged to transform their schools into learning communities that provide students and staff with a renewed sense of meaning and purpose to their work. We write this book with confidence that transformational leadership is possible, for we believe that the talent and dedication for a transformational model of leadership are widely distributed among current and aspiring school leaders. We are confident, as well, that those who prepare future leaders for these transformational roles have the talent and moral commitment to prepare them well. As we view the landscape of administrator preparation, we are encouraged to find laboratories for such learning already present in the form of learning communities, both formally and informally structured. These learning communities are natural settings for students to experience both content and process curriculum.

In many cases, learning communities have been formalized in instructional settings called cohorts, cooperative-learning groups, problem-based learning groups, or teams. In other situations, learning communities have evolved spontaneously within regular educational settings as dedicated professors and engaged students have formed alliances or networks for learning and research, or as students themselves have formed study groups. In all cases, these settings provide opportunities for students to experience and internalize important values and concepts about community and to understand more directly the role that leaders play in fostering it.

The impact on learning varies, for not all groups are true learning communities. In this book, we recount our own experiences with groups of adult students, or cohorts, that we have worked with in our universities during the past few years. Based on our research and experience with these cohorts, we are confident in calling them "learning communities." Our major premise is that when students are prepared for leadership in true learning communities, they are involved in unique learning laboratories where they are provided opportunities to obtain the dispositions, knowledge, and performance skills to become transformational leaders.

BACKGROUND

We have explored learning communities from many vantage points. As a research team, we have been engaged in the study of learning communities, inspired by the enhanced learning and personal empowerment of our own students as they have lived and learned within communities. We also have been involved in a learning community of our own. We are avid believers in the power of the learning community process.

Our Interest in Learning Communities

Initially, our work with learning communities was in five separate universities: the Universities of Indiana, Houston, Wyoming, and Northern Colorado, and California State University, Fresno. More recently, our work has extended to the University of Tennessee and San Diego State University. During the past 10 years of research and teaching, we have worked collectively with over 2,500 students who have lived and learned within community settings called cohorts. Although our individual learning communities have been structured in a variety of ways, they have all contained some basic commonalities that make them comparable.

First, all have been part of graduate programs in educational leadership focusing on the preparation of school leaders. Second, students have remained together for a large portion of their programs, taking the same classes and working with a small cadre of professors who have, under some conditions and in some places, also operated as learning communities. Third, students in these learning settings have been taught in nontraditional fashion characterized by problem-based learning approaches, reflective activities, field-based studies and internships, personal awareness opportunities, and values clarification experiences. In all situations, the curriculum has been designed with an emphasis on adult learning theory and a constructivist approach to learning. Finally, during their learning process, many students have kept detailed accounts of their impressions, typically constructed in the form of reflective journals. These journals have ranged in format from daily written journal entries to weekly e-mail reflections.

In this book, we recount what we have learned about learning communities through our students' perceptions and our own experiences and research. Some of our information has been gleaned from formal studies and some from reflections collected informally. Because we have completed several formal studies on our cohorts, we provide some background on these investigations.

The first study, completed in 1994, was based on data from reflective journals of 51 students across four universities (Norris & Barnett, 1994), providing us with the initial structure of the cohort model described in Chapter 1. The second study, a follow-up of 100 additional student journals (Norris, Herrmond, & Meisgeier, 1996) from these same universities, expanded our earlier findings and refined our conceptual model. The third study, comprising 150 students from the University of Houston, investigated students' creative thinking and learning within a cohort setting (Norris, Herrmond, & Meisgeier, 1996), which gave us insight into the knowledge acquisition of students within cohort settings. A fourth study examined the effectiveness of a district-level cohort (Norris, Hooker, Weise, & Baitland, 1996) and expanded the concept of a learning community beyond the confines of the university setting. A final qualitative study looked at the transfer of students' expressed values to their actions in the workplace (Norris, Barnett, Basom, & Yerkes, 1996). In Chapter 3 of this book, we present four case studies from our investigation. We have explored the use of cohorts (as possible learning communities) in educational leadership programs across the United States and Canada (Barnett, Basom, Yerkes, & Norris, 2000). We share some of our impressions from this study in Chapter 6 as we examine the current trends and future directions of university-based learning communities.

In addition to our writing team's own studies of cohort programs, three doctoral students from the University of Houston also completed dissertations based on the initial learning community (cohort) at the University of Houston (Baitland, 1992; Lebsack, 1993; Weise, 1992). These studies, too, added greatly to our understandings of the cohort processes and their continuing evolution.

All of these research studies have influenced our thinking as we have developed the conceptual frameworks and the learning community model presented in this book. (The reader is referred to these original studies for a more detailed explanation of our methodology and findings.) Our early impressions focused on group dynamics literature; however, we expanded our conceptualization to include the literature addressing learning communities, transformational leadership, ethics and values, learning transfer, change theory, curriculum theory, and personality theory. From a synthesis of these sources, our conceptual framework emerged.

History of Our Journey Together

As a research team, we began our exploration of educational administration cohorts in the early 1990s under the sponsorship of the Danforth Foundation, based in St. Louis, Missouri. For several years prior to becoming a research team, each of us had served as Danforth facilitators for our respective universities. As facilitators, we studied leadership preparation, learned from the experts and each other, planned and tested new ideas, made connections with excellent faculty from across the United States, and strove to improve our own programs. As faculty members from over 25 universities from across the nation, we were, ourselves, the beginnings of a learning community.

In 1993, when the Danforth Foundation's financial and organizational support for our collective efforts to improve the education of future school administrators was coming to a close, the four of us accepted the challenge to continue our work through cross-university collaboration. Armed with a small initiation grant from the Foundation, we began our journey to study and learn more about cohorts.

The universities involved in the Danforth initiative had designed their programs using a cohort delivery model, primarily because of the structural feasibility and convenience this arrangement provided. Many Danforth programs were at that time exploratory pilots, operating as supplementary preparation programs within more traditional university settings. Since we had worked in these cohorts over a period of time, we had come to believe that there were other benefits to the cohort system aside from structure and convenience. It became our desire to investigate what was happening to students within these cohorts and to explore more fully the benefits that might be derived from cohort settings. We believed, too, that a conceptual framework needed to be developed that would provide a greater sense of direction to curriculum content and delivery within the cohort. And so, our investigation of cohorts as a collaborative research team was launched.

If the four of us had known when we started our journey together what we know today, we might have kept journals, done more reflecting, and designed our work together more deliberately. Instead, we set out, without a clear roadmap, to study the groups of students in our educational leadership preparation programs that we then called "cohorts."

Our journey first took us to a literature review on group dynamics, the concept of cohorts in other fields, sociological and psychological perspectives on groups, groups in education and counseling, curriculum, and leadership. Over time, we began to refine our sense of cohorts, writing and presenting our ideas about how adults learn and grow within group settings. We conducted the research mentioned earlier and convened groups of interested faculty at national meetings to talk about what we were learning and inquire about their experiences with groups they were calling cohorts.

We initially thought we were studying the cohort—known to some as no more than a convenient device for scheduling students. We soon found that we were studying far more than student groupings that seemed to work. Nevertheless, the roadmap unfolded only as the journey continued. Gradually, we began to see that we really were talking about leadership, learning, teaching, and community. It also became clear to us that there had to be productive ways to help graduate students transfer their own learning and experiences to the worlds in which they would work—the administrative offices and hallways and classrooms of schools.

This book, the culmination of our journey, is written from a desire to share what we have learned along the way. We hope that in so doing we encourage more thoughtful attention to the design, delivery, and transfer of student learning that can, and does, take place in educational settings. Our journey will be rewarded if those who read this book have a greater interest in using learning communities as laboratories for leadership preparation.

ORGANIZATION OF BOOK

The first four chapters present the theoretical basis for learning communities, connect values clarification to leader and community development, present case studies demonstrating transfer of espoused theory (articulated values) to theory in use (leadership behavior), and discuss transactional and transformational leadership in relation to the knowledge base of educational administration. Chapters 5 and 6 provide a framework for content and process curriculum, discuss the transfer of learning to work settings, and examine emerging trends and issues concerning learning communities.

Chapter 1 develops the concept of a learning community as both a structure for the delivery of course content (the product) and a laboratory for promoting collaborative or transformational leadership values (the process). Based on empirical findings from our own work, we present a learning community model, emphasizing group and individual development.

The learning community concept, from a sociological perspective, is built around three essential components: interaction, purpose, and interdependence. The individual, or psychological, perspective is based on empirical findings from our own work suggesting that individual development takes place according to sequential growth stages of: (1) support, (2) security, (3) friendship, (4) knowledge acquisition, and (5) realization of the personal dream.

In Chapter 2, we take the position that leadership is developed in a hierarchical fashion through phases of values awareness. We use Hall's

(1976) theory of values consciousness as a lens for exploring the developmental nature of values acquisition and for presenting the phases essential to leadership development. The effect that values have on shaping organizational context is explained through a discussion of three organizational metaphors: machines, organisms, and brains (Morgan, 1986). These metaphorical lenses of organizational context are compared with the historical stages of leadership preparation (the scientific management stage, the technological/human relations stage, and the human resources/systems stage). We conclude by suggesting that the philosophy underlying administrator preparation either directs future leaders toward the acquisition of higher phases of values consciousness (transformational leadership perspectives) or perpetuates lower phases of values consciousness equated with directive (transactional leadership) approaches. The culminating point of this chapter demonstrates how the learning community model introduced in Chapter 1 supports Hall's higher levels of values consciousness and provides students with the means for actualizing their values goals, thereby enhancing their leadership development.

Chapter 3 examines the relationship between school leaders' espoused theory and values (as articulated during their learning community experience) and their theory in use (as demonstrated in their actions as school leaders). Leadership platforms (Barnett, 1992), in which future leaders articulated their personal beliefs and values and created their personal dreams (Levinson, 1986), are used to reveal their theories in use. Leadership portraitures (Lightfoot, 1983), developed from four case studies of practicing school leaders, each a former member of a learning community, are used to examine this issue.

These portraitures compare the values that former cohort students espoused during their leadership preparation with the values that they espoused later in their practice. Espoused values, expressed in their leadership platforms and later in personal interviews, are compared with each individual's theory in use determined from the perceptions of staff members during focused interviews. Their values also are explored and analyzed using Hall's (1976) theory of values consciousness and Morgan's (1986) metaphors of organizations, introduced in Chapter 2.

In Chapter 4, we explore the theories of transactional and transformational leadership. The eternal conflict between management and leadership is examined by considering the question: Are transactional and transformational leadership two sides of the same coin (Bass, 1985; Sergiovanni, 1992), or are they opposite ends of a continuum (Burns, 1978; Foster, 1986)? Central to this question is an exploration of "servant leadership" (Greenleaf, 1977) and the moral dimensions such leadership entails. A leadership continuum is proposed: (1) transactional leadership—the managerial behavior of the designated leader; (2) transactional and transformational leadership—a value-added form of leadership orchestrated from a contingency leadership approach; and (3) transformational leadership—a proactive, questioning leadership style dedicated to individual and organizational renewal. The components of this leadership continuum are related to previous discussions of values consciousness, metaphorical organizational contexts, leadership preparation stages, and learning communities.

Chapter 5 introduces the nature of the leadership development curriculum delivered within a learning community setting. Curriculum is shown to have a dual purpose: (1) to present the content, or knowledge base, that provides a contextual understanding of the arena in which educational leadership is enacted, and (2) to explore and inform the process of developing a learning community with the idea of promoting the development of leadership skills and their application to school settings.

The content curriculum, or knowledge base of educational administration, is described through the lens of standards, or frameworks, that serve as springboards for exploring and classifying the knowledge, dispositions, and performances expected of effective school leaders. The process curriculum, or experienced learning related to the learning community itself, occurs as a natural outgrowth of the cohort experience. We examine various instruction applications conducted within learning communities and relate them to the leadership continuum and values consciousness phases described earlier.

In Chapter 6, we discuss the ultimate goal, or legacy, of learning communities: the development of transformational leaders who possess higher levels of values consciousness, are capable of empowering others, and can inspire community. We discuss the urgent need for future leaders to transfer their learning to practice so that organizations and individuals can benefit from the transformational nature of learning communities. This chapter focuses on the concepts of learning transfer and the application of those concepts to leadership skill transfer. Broad-based research on the nature of learning transfer is presented. Using these research findings, connections are made between key learning transfer principles and reflective practice, which must take place during the community-building process if learning transfer is to occur. Chapter 6 also raises points for reflection and discussion relative to the formation of learning communities and the benefits that these communities provide to those concerned with the preparation of school leaders. Emerging trends are considered and questions are raised for future practice and research.

We conclude our exploration of learning communities with an epilogue in which we describe our personal experiences as a cohort, despite working in different universities. We share impressions of our own development, using growth stages reflected in our learning community model. Since the reward system in higher education perpetuates individuality, it is a bit unusual to work as a learning community. For this reason we believe it is important to share our experiences as a developing learning community.

1

The Learning Community

Individuals are intricately interwoven into groups and groups are reflections of individuals. Individuals are supported, affirmed, and inspired in groups; they are transformed. In turn, individuals transform groups through their collective efforts and commitment to a meaningful purpose. Groups empower individuals; individuals empower groups. It is a reciprocal process known as COMMUNITY.

—Cynthia J. Norris and Bruce G. Barnett

COMMUNITY CELEBRATES the dignity and worth of self and others, fosters the empowerment of both, and encourages and supports the maximum development of human potential for the benefit of the common good. The very word *community* implies unity, relationship, and a kindred sense of spirit. The concept of relationship is central to the definition, for it suggests an emotional bonding resulting from the interaction of individuals joined in a common purpose. In a learning community the purpose is "learning"; therefore, individual and collective growth are the products of that relationship.

This book is about the development of learning communities; it is concerned, as well, with the development of leaders who will transform their schools into such settings. We suggest that as future leaders experience community, they learn to speak the language of community, learn to build connections that foster community, and, most important, learn to value community—not only for themselves, but also for others. Throughout this book, we challenge those who prepare future leaders to consider learning communities as laboratories for providing them with the *dispositions*, *knowledge*, and *performance* skills necessary for fostering learning communities within their future schools.

This chapter begins by providing a list of assumptions or belief statements that support this book. We then consider the need for learning communities by examining examples of disenfranchisement in school settings contrasted with the benefits of personal empowerment afforded through community. Next, based on our own studies of learning communities, we present a learning community model that serves as a guide for shaping other chapters throughout this book. We conclude this chapter by casting our model within the context of learning community literature and suggesting implications for those responsible for designing preparation programs for school leaders. We begin our discussion by presenting the belief statements and assumptions that frame our work.

BELIEF STATEMENTS AND ASSUMPTIONS

We have only begun to understand the power of the learning community. We have, however, formed some vivid impressions, or belief statements, as a result of our work. These statements serve as the underlying assumptions on which our learning communities rest, as well as the basic assumptions of this book. From our work with learning communities, we have come to believe that:

1. Knowledge and acceptance of self and others, along with a willingness to share power through collective contributions, is the foundation of community.
2. An ethic of care surrounds a true learning community.
3. Personal awareness and values acquisition are dependent not only on knowledge of but on experiences with others. Experience is the greatest teacher.
4. Learning communities exert a powerful influence in shaping personal and collective values.
5. Learning communities are laboratories for experiencing transformational leadership and for forming the dispositions, knowledge, and performance skills necessary for transformational leadership.
6. A learning community *structure* (a cohort or team) does not automatically ensure that a learning community will evolve.
7. Professors can inhibit the full development of learning communities, as well as the benefits derived from them, by their insistence on maintaining a "sage on the stage" model of instruction.
8. Transfer of learning must be purposefully reinforced throughout the learning community experience if the dispositions, knowledge, and performance of future leaders are to be enacted.

A consideration of learning communities requires an understanding of their need. Why are learning community experiences important in developing future leaders? Why, in fact, is there a need to develop leaders who can fashion such communities? Past and present conditions within our schools speak vividly to this issue.

THE NEED FOR LEARNING COMMUNITIES

Feelings of isolation and disengagement experienced by many in today's schools stifle their full development and limit organizational performance. Students, teachers, parents, and administrators manifest these feelings in a variety of ways. Among the student population, they are evidenced by the burgeoning increase in student underachievement—even among the gifted and talented populations—and in a steady incline in the dropout rate that seems to cut across all intellectual, racial, and economic levels (Strain, 1993). They are expressed in aberrant behavioral patterns, including truancy, drug abuse, and gang-related problems (Blankstein & Sandoval, 1998; Freed, 1999; Trueba, Spindler, & Spindler, 1989). Perhaps less obvious, but just as debilitating to student potential, are those situations in which students "go through the motions" and endure in quiet desperation.

Among the teaching staff, disenfranchisement is seen in the mass exodus of young teachers after their first year of teaching (Holland & Weise, 1999) and in burnout among more "seasoned" staff (Cunningham, 1983; Dworkin, 1987; Farber, 1984; Maslach, 1982). Disengagement, too, is reflected in incompetence, lack of motivation, insecurity or lack of confidence, absenteeism, and resignation (Goodlad, 1984; Little, 1993; Shaw, 1981).

Parents, too, often feel disenfranchised and are hesitant to become involved in their children's education (National Center for Education Statistics, 1998). The problem with lack of parental involvement is increased in settings of low socioeconomics and ethnic diversity, where a major chasm often exists between the home and the school.

Even some administrators have their own problems with disengagement. Some express feelings of loneliness, isolation, or hopelessness in the work setting, while others seek relief through school transfer, early retirement, or career change (Marshall & Kasten, 1994).

In most cases of disenfranchisement, individuals have lost their sense of identity with the organization. They feel cut off from the real purpose and business of the enterprise and react in silence as others carry on the business of education. There is a great need in our schools to bring back the joy of learning for all and a renewed sense of being part of something important and meaningful.

Problems wrought by disenfranchisement are, of course, not always easy to solve. The key to their resolution often lies in finding ways to provide individuals with that sense of belonging considered to be the overarching goal of all human beings (Dreikurs, Grunwald, & Peppers, 1982). Many believe that membership in a true community provides the best avenue for fulfilling this need.

The challenge of building community does not rest with the schools alone. Educational administration programs, too, need to foster a new leadership paradigm that embraces community. Not only should they model community among themselves, but they also should view their students as communities of learners and leaders. They should ensure that future leaders are provided with the tools necessary for creating collaborative-learning environments in their schools. Leadership preparation needs to be *process-* as well as *content-*driven, with university community settings serving as laboratories in which collaborative leadership is examined and refined.

PERSONAL EMPOWERMENT THROUGH LEARNING COMMUNITIES

Gardner (1989) reminds us that where community exists, members feel an identity and sense of belonging that fosters security. He adds that ideals of justice and compassion are nurtured in communities, as they were in an earlier era when personal support came not only from one's family but also from an extended family or the community. Those who seek the notion of community today believe that it embodies the best of contemporary values, is inclusive, balances individual freedom and group obligation, fosters the release of human potential, and invites sharing and participation in leadership tasks. Such are the characteristics of personal empowerment.

Empowerment, then, grows out of community. The term *empowerment* is closely related to the idea of self-actualization and can be defined as a sense of having control or influence over one's own life and circumstances and over the decisions that affect one's life. Empowered individuals express this inner freedom through increased spontaneity and confidence in their own personal abilities and by exhibiting an openness and receptivity to life (Maslow, 1976).

The idea of empowerment is supported by three important theories identified by Louis E. Rath: the theory of needs, the theory of values, and the theory of thinking (Wasserman, 1991). Certainly, Gardner (1989) touches on all three of these theories in his description of a true learning community. We consider each theory as it relates to empowerment.

The theory of *needs* (Alderfer, 1972; Herzberg, 1968; Maslow, 1976; McClellan, 1976) is basic to the formation of a learning community. Most writers view physical and emotional security needs as the foundation for other higher-level needs, such as the needs for belonging, achievement, self-esteem, and self-actualization. Each need identified by the researchers above appears to match a need expressed by our students and to be reflected in the learning community model presented later in this chapter. Our studies add to the body of literature, suggesting that learning communities do seem to promote a sense of emotional security and that this need is more likely to be fulfilled in situations where individuals feel that they have a support group. Our research also suggests that other needs of the individual, such as the needs for belonging, achievement, and self-actualization, are fulfilled within community.

A second theory that supports empowerment is the *values* theory. In Chapters 2 and 3 we discuss the importance of leaders being aware of their own values and visions. It is difficult for leaders to lead with credibility and to inspire others' commitment to a shared purpose if they do not have a clear sense of their own values and purpose. Future leaders need opportunities to clarify their values, to share in the development of personal visions and platforms, and to formulate collective visions for group efforts. In Chapter 5 we provide a full discussion of curriculum and instructional methods that foster values clarification.

Finally, the theory of *thinking* has a major impact on setting conditions for individual empowerment. Research indicates that learning is greatly enhanced in learning communities when students are provided opportunities to share ideas, to elaborate on their own thoughts, and to consider the ideas of others (Brubaker, 1994; Norris & Barnett, 1994; Norris, Herrmond, & Meisgeier, 1996; Senge, 1990). As our students have noted, a community atmosphere provides the climate for free exchange of ideas and critical analysis of issues. Professors can provide such opportunities through problem-based learning activities, study groups, discussions, and group projects—methods that we discuss in greater detail in Chapter 5. It is important to note here, however, that before empowerment can happen, there must be leaders who are skilled in the development of communities and leaders (and professors) who value the collaboration and interdependence gained through human involvement.

LEARNING COMMUNITIES CONCEPTUALIZED

When individuals form groups to accomplish any objective, they are immediately confronted with a problem: How do they appropriately blend *task* and *relationship* (Hersey & Blanchard, 1982; Tannenbaum & Schmidt, 1958)? How do leaders accomplish the objectives of the group or organization and, at the same time, "provide work climates where individuals are inspired to develop their own potentialities, become self-empowered, and contribute creatively to the enhancement of the organization" (Norris, Basom, Yerkes, & Barnett, 1996, p. 145)? Another way of expressing this same dilemma is to ask: How can the needs of the group be met without sacrificing the needs of the individual—or vice versa? If Barnard's (1968a) claim that leadership is the catalyst that provides individual and group cooperation is accurate, then future leaders must be inspired to become such catalysts. How they learn the skills and develop the attitudes or dispositions necessary to become transformational leaders will be our consideration in the remainder of this chapter. Understanding the nature of groups and individuals within those groups is an important place to begin.

SOCIOLOGICAL AND PSYCHOLOGICAL NATURE OF GROUPS

Groups are both sociological and psychological in nature. Their sociological dimension is concerned with how the group itself develops and how it, in turn, interfaces with other groups. Applied to university preparation settings, then, the learning community structure (possibly a cohort) would be considered a group that interfaces with many other individuals and groups such as professors, field-based mentors, district-level personnel, other students, and professional groups within education. Although proximity and a shared or common purpose would indicate a true group, it is interdependence that is the true hallmark of a genuine group. Interdependence results from face-to-face interaction and communication, coupled with a shared purpose (Cartwright, 1968; Hare, 1952; McGrath & Altman, 1966). In summary, there are four specific qualities that denote a genuine group.

First, a dynamic *interaction* takes place among group members. This interaction can be facilitated in several ways, such as by the size of the group (an optimal size being 20–25) and the frequency and quality of the interaction. Positive involvement and accountability are further intensified by frequent interaction among group members (Johnson & Johnson, 1987). In university settings, this interaction is intensified to the extent that the professor removes him- or herself from center stage and allows students to focus their attention on each other and on the group (Loeser, 1957). In Chapter 5 we discuss the critical role that the professor plays in fostering this interdependence through more nontraditional instructional approaches, such as problem-based learning and study groups.

A second feature of a true group is that the members work together toward a unified *purpose*. Again, it is important that leaders facilitate rather than direct this process. The more students can determine their own purposes in the learning process, the more likely they are to work together toward the set goals. A sense of purpose develops when mutual interactions and collaboration take place (Zander, 1982).

The third quality of a true group is *interdependence*. Collaboration and interaction promote a group identity or cohesiveness that is evidenced by the quantity and quality of communication (Shaw, 1981) and by member satisfaction within the group.

Last, in cohesive groups, individuals show respect for one another and a real appreciation and acknowledgment of their individual differences and contributions. A sense of security results within this environment that allows and promotes a free exchange of ideas with no fear of retribution or disfavor. In such a setting, there is *individual growth*. Individuals receive mutual feedback in a safe environment, become more self-aware, and develop greater knowledge through dialogue with others (Senge, 1990). As individuals grow, their contributions strengthen the effectiveness of the entire group. Interdependent groups establish their identity, set norms for behavior of group members, and influence one another's direction (Johnson & Johnson, 1987).

Based on our studies of learning communities, we have found that our cohorts were indeed true groups that manifested these four qualities. We share with you excerpts from an earlier published article reporting the results of one of these studies; it lends support to the literature on group process (Norris, Barnett, Basom, & Yerkes, 1996).

REVIEW OF THE STUDY

The concepts discussed in this chapter are based on studies of educational administration cohorts in four universities: Houston, Northern Colorado, Wyoming, and California at Fresno. The first study, completed in 1994, was based on data collected from 51 subjects across the four universities (Norris & Barnett, 1994). A second study collected data from 100 additional students from these four sites (Norris, Basom, Yerkes, & Barnett, 1996). In this chapter, we discuss student perceptions gleaned from these two studies. In both studies, students kept detailed journals of their experiences in learning communities. Each student, at the end of the program, submitted a summary of important insights he or she had gained throughout the program. These journal summaries were analyzed and coded into major categories, including individual growth, group growth, interaction, process, transferability, advantages, and disadvantages. Using the constant comparative method of analysis (Glaser, 1965), we further broke down comments relating to either group or individual development into subcategories. (Readers are referred to the original studies for a more detailed description of the methodology employed.) For our purposes in this chapter, we will consider student comments that pertained to two of the above categories: group development and individual development.

GROUP DEVELOPMENT: THE SOCIOLOGICAL PERSPECTIVE

Student comments indicate that the students perceived their learning communities to be interdependent, fully functioning groups rather than mere collections of individuals placed together for scheduling convenience. They expressed their feelings about group development in these comments:

> I never expected to see the quality of fellowship and friendship-building activities as I witnessed this summer. . . . It will last a lifetime . . . I thought it was not possible after youth. It is indeed possible.

> The most important aspect was being able to build a family tree to fall back on later.

> I think we have really grown and come together to bond as a group.

> We have become much closer and respectful of each other's talents.

They recognized that through interaction they increased their comfort level in working together. As they expressed it:

> Interaction strengthened relationships and helped ease anxieties through sharing of experiences.

> We learned to share knowledge, participate in the group process by dividing the work, and brought excellent efforts to the final project.

> We developed in a positive way.

Not only did the group members feel a spirit of connectedness, but they also perceived that the group worked together toward the accomplishment of goals. There was a purpose, which united members in common pursuit. As they indicated:

> Diversity with a common purpose is powerful. That is a belief statement of our cohort that stands out for me.

> Presentations forced me to work together to accomplish a common goal.

> Evidence of group cooperation and a sense of enjoyment prevailed as the groups made their presentations.

> We were less concerned with our grades and more concerned with the importance of the tasks.

Bonding took place within these learning communities, a finding that confirms much of the earlier research about cohesiveness within university cohort programs (Herbert & Reynolds, n.d.; Hill, 1992; Kasten, 1992). The mutual support and solidarity found in other groups (Johnson & Johnson, 1987) seemed to permeate the feelings expressed by the students in these learning communities. Many of the words they used to describe their feelings had a striking resemblance to the terms used in the earlier studies. Repeatedly we encountered in their journals such terms as "close relationships," "family tree," "bonding," "inclusion," and "community." We were left with the impression that these students genuinely liked each other and valued the time spent in their learning experience. One student expressed it this way:

> The most important aspect of my cohort experience has been the sense of teamwork and each group member having responsibility for bringing a piece of the complete puzzle.

From the learning community experience, some insight is gained regarding students' understanding of the factors that promoted or hindered cohesiveness. They suggested that they were inspired to bond together by such things as "time availability," "modeling," "out of class activities," "varied activities," and "a chance to talk about what we were experiencing." Professor attitude was also important. As various students noted:

Our cohort professor let us create, test, and search on our own. That's the toughest but most meaningful part.

The structure of the course forced us to get to know one another better, listen to each other, and trust one another.

The instructor was skilled in guiding and encouraging the group.

Students captured the feelings of interdependence that seemed to pervade these learning communities:

As we spoke to each other in discussions and self-disclosed, an interesting event occurred. It happened without our direct knowledge and came quietly into each of our lives. The group became almost like an extension of each of us because we all brought a part of ourselves and exposed our most inner thoughts to those in the group.

The cohort produced such synergy that if we could have bottled it, we could have taken the show on the road.

Students felt that two important factors increased their cohesiveness: spending time planning group projects and actually participating in joint presentations. As they indicated:

Groupwork enabled us to recognize and utilize each other's strengths, thereby contributing to our growing sense of community.

Presentations forced us to work together to accomplish a common goal.

Working as a group on our project and sharing ideas about the material in the text were the key factors in developing our ability to work together.

The cohorts' interdependence was exemplified by members' perceived ability to resolve emerging problems. Rather than depending on the instructors to resolve problems or being passive themselves, cohort members sensed that their strength lay in being able to deal constructively with the problems and challenges that arose. These feelings are best reflected in these reactions:

We were trying to work out a schedule; it was obvious that we had moved into the storming stage. We were able to argue and get upset, but once it was over, we were upset at the actions, but not the people.

Some in the group realized "pulling their load" is a responsibility and not a suggestion. . . . It forced the group to figure out ways to work effectively.

Of course, these feelings were not always positive and growth producing. Students did identify certain factors that inhibited collaboration. They would have preferred more balanced contributions by all group members and were bothered when some of their classmates did not participate equally. They reveal these frustrations in some of the following comments:

The dynamics of our group have been very interesting to observe. I still feel that we need to identify some ways to reach out to the quieter members of our group.

Our group had a tough time in the last 2 days of IPR because of a few people speaking up after many weeks of silence.

The quality of interaction between the students has been superior! After the initial turmoil died down, we got along very well and stayed on task throughout each class session.

For the most part, though, the students appreciated the opportunity to be involved in a process they found productive, and they perceived growth in the total group as a result of the experience. As they explained:

The cohort has grown closer . . . we feel more comfortable with each other . . . we've learned each other's strengths and weaknesses.

The cohort has developed into a culture. We all care about each other as if we are all family.

INDIVIDUAL DEVELOPMENT: THE PSYCHOLOGICAL PERSPECTIVE

From experience in working with these learning communities and from the impressions they have shared, it appears that individual development within a learning community proceeds through a continuum of developmental stages. The inner triangle displayed in Figure 1.1 shows the perceived growth of these individuals. The outer triangle represents the perceived growth of the group. While all students may not reach the highest stage of individual development, the progression toward full development seems to proceed in a similar fashion for all. The development stages identified in our work include: (1) support, (2) security, (3) friendship, (4) knowledge acquisition, and (5) personal dream (Norris, Basom, Yerkes, & Barnett, 1996). Students' impressions regarding their own development within each of these stages will now be discussed.

Support

Graduate students in these learning communities expressed the belief that significant individual growth did take place as a result of their experience. They indicated that the group supported them—"made them feel connected and not isolated." They "sought out one another to find solutions" and "pulled together to see the task through." They talked about the sharing that took place:

> We learned how to use individual strengths to benefit the whole group.

> I felt like the coursework seemed overwhelming at first. But with the help of the other group members, we were able to complete it successfully. I learned so much in the process.

> The feeling of support and having others to reassure us when we felt like quitting were important aspects of my cohort experience.

> Being in a group with the same people and learning to work with them and have their support has been very important to me.

Security

These learning communities seemed to provide a climate for trust that allowed individual members to become more emotionally secure. This nurturing atmosphere seemed to foster individual freedom to feel "validated," "secure," and "connected," and to experience "risk-taking" and a "questioning stance." Many in the community expressed these feelings:

> We have all risked things with each other and we all feel good about it.

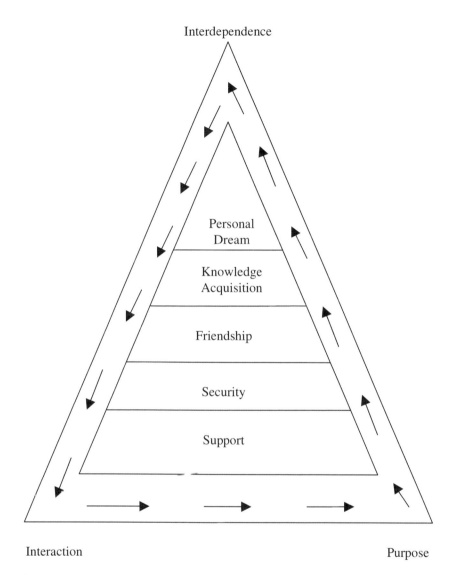

Figure 1.1. The cohort model.

We are friends now and I expect that friendship to strengthen.

The environment in the class allowed me to feel secure enough to venture out and trust. This was a big step for me.

There was tremendous growth in the trust level of the group that allowed individuals the opportunity to question and experiment in a caring environment.

The group became almost like an extension of each of us.

Friendship

The mutual support and solidarity found in effective groups seemed to have permeated the feelings expressed by these students. Repeatedly, throughout the journal summaries, words such as "close relationship," "family tree," "bonding," "fellowship," "acceptance," "inclusion," "community," and "empowerment" are found. Wrapped in these community climates, individuals appear to have responded to the warmth and concern they felt were extended. In turn, individuals reached out to others. Friendship bonds were formed. Individuals acknowledged personal feelings of "tolerance," "acceptance," and "care" for others. One is left with the impression that these students genuinely liked each other and valued the time spent in their cohort learning experience. Comments such as the following exemplify these attitudes:

I started to care about these people.

I enjoyed getting to know people who have the same hopes and dreams I have.

The most important aspect has been appreciating the different personalities. I have become more flexible.

I learned to value the opinions of others as being important and valid contributions to the project being worked on.

We have all learned a lot from each other and care for each other very much.

As we spoke to each other in discussions and self-disclosed, an interesting event occurred. It happened without our direct knowledge and came quietly into each of our lives. I believe that immediate trust, true concern for each other, and a bonding of sorts took place naturally and with ease.

In a climate of community empowerment, these future leaders appear to have learned the important skills and lessons necessary for promoting cooperation in the organizations they will one day lead.

Knowledge Acquisition

Students in these learning communities indicated that their knowledge and understanding were greatly enhanced through their group experiences in the leadership preparation program. Several students mentioned this as a significant factor in their personal development. They talked of "learning with meaning," "relevance," "self-direction," and "application of theory to reality" as being important characteristics of their learning experience. They did not view their learning as complete, however, but mentioned the words "challenge," "determined," "building upon," and "committed" as they discussed their zeal to continue their development. Their comments suggested that the experience of working in a cohesive group was meaningful:

> Group projects were very beneficial and the application was much more meaningful than knowledge-level lectures.

> I learned more from the group by debating ideas. Having others to bounce ideas off of was a good experience.

> The groupwork was excellent because we were forced to come to grips with difficult information, agree on the decisions made, and then be under the gun to organize and present in a professional manner.

> By being in a cohort, I was able to see different points of view that I may never have seen in a traditional classroom. I learned more as a result. It was extremely helpful having others to share interpretations with. By discussing our own views, we were able to gain confidence when our own points were accepted and learn when others disagreed.

> Much of what I intuitively knew was made more clear to me by being so well thought out and expressed. It really helped me to clarify and to solidify some of my perceptions.

The Personal Dream

Students in these communities acknowledged the growth in self-aware-ness that was afforded them through the group interaction. The develop-ment of leadership artistry requires that future leaders come to terms with their own personal beliefs and values as part of that personal under-standing. Comments such as the following indicate that many experienced this awareness:

> The growth that I have experienced has been profound. . . . I knew what I could do, but I really didn't know who I was. . . . I learned to define my internal core. Understanding who I am keeps me out of the box in which I allowed too many people to place me. I now live on a mountain of my own making. . . . My perch has become a vantage point from which I can celebrate being alive.

> A powerful transformation has taken place in my life.

> I truly have made many self-discoveries. . . . Many things that I sus-pected about myself and my leadership style have been reaf-firmed.

> I have learned a lot about my leadership potential and gained con-fidence in my abilities.

> The atmosphere of the class seemed to bring on a real sense of un-derstanding.

A LEARNING COMMUNITY MODEL

These characteristics of individual and group development form the framework of our learning community model shown in Figure 1.1. This is a conceptual model based on our review of the literature of group dynamics and our own experiences with learning communities. We be-lieve there is some value in testing this model, and we present it here, not only as a work in progress, but also in the hope that it will encourage others to examine and test it further.

The inner triangle in this model represents the individuals within the educational administration learning community. The outer rim of the triangle represents the community as a total group. The group is built on three major cornerstones, each influencing and strengthening the others.

Those cornerstones are: interaction (results in cohesiveness among group members), purpose (promotes collaboration), and interdependence (results from cohesiveness and represents the hallmark of a true group). The model is cyclic in the sense that each point in the group's progressive development continues to be reinforced by the steps that preceded it.

As demonstrated by the model's inner triangle, the individual is encased within the supportive climate of the group. As the group is strengthened, the individual, too, experiences growth. That growth proceeds systematically in the sense that each step toward full development is a growth area, or need, that group membership promotes for the individual. As these needs, or growth areas (support, security, friendship, knowledge acquisition) are fulfilled, the individual moves in an upward pathway toward realization of the personal dream, or view of self in the world (Levinson, 1986). It is the personal dream that forms the basis of leadership artistry, a concept we will develop in Chapter 2.

It is important to note that even though these developmental steps are viewed as hierarchical, the needs felt at each step continue to permeate the individual's life and future development. Each step continues to reinforce the others. The individual's total development within the learning community is enhanced as the group itself is strengthened.

The final point is perhaps most significant of all. The further the individual progresses in the hierarchy, or is empowered, the more significantly the individual contributes to the development of the group. Empowered individuals empower groups. As groups are empowered, so are individuals. It is a celebration of interdependency transforming both the individual and the community.

The ultimate benefit of this leadership development process is reflected in an additional triangle extending from the first, as shown in Figure 1.2. As the student is empowered through the learning community experience, the knowledge and skills acquired should transfer to form the foundation for the transformational leadership necessary for promoting future empowered leaders within schools.

IMPLICATIONS FOR SCHOOL LEADERSHIP

Growth and self-renewal are the cornerstones of a learning community. If we consider schools as learning communities, it stands to reason that school principals must be "responsible for *building organizations* where people are continually expanding their capabilities to shape their future— that is leaders are responsible for learning" (Senge, 1990, p. 9). Learning should not be viewed merely as achievement at a certain level of compe-

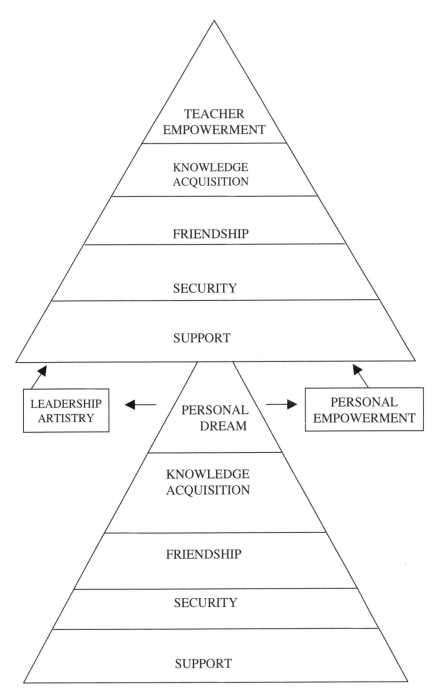

Figure 1.2. Transformational leadership through community.

tency; rather it should be perceived as an attitude of lifelong growth and development. Learning organizations never "fully arrive." Their self-actualized spirit keeps them ever searching for new possibilities and opportunities for growth. Five important dimensions characterize learning communities: personal mastery, mental models, shared values, team learning, and systems thinking (Senge, 1990). We relate those five dimensions to the model of learning communities previously presented and to the impressions shared by our students. We begin by considering the concept of personal mastery.

Personal Mastery

Consideration of the term *personal mastery* focuses our attention on what learning truly means. Learning requires more than just dealing in the cognitive realm of understanding, for although personal mastery is based on competence and skill, it extends the domains of knowledge to include personal relevance and meaning. Values and personal meaning become integrated with acquired knowledge, resulting in a drawing forth rather than a handing down of knowledge.

Senge (1990) suggests that personal mastery is learning how to deal with *creative tension*, a concept that he defines as the gap between what one cognitively and affectively knows *should be* with the reality of *what is*. This tension provides a creative spark that causes one to extend acquired knowledge and strive to become all that one is capable of being. Personal mastery is the quality that gives individuals a sense of belonging to and ownership in an organization. It is the "spiritual foundation" that provides not only purpose and passion, but also commitment to the work of the organization and to one's own individual development (Senge, 1990).

Personal mastery brings meaning to life, since it is learning that enables individuals to get in touch with themselves and what they have to contribute. In that sense, it is much akin to the notion of the personal dream (Levinson, 1986), or view of self in the world—a notion incorporated into the learning community model previously presented. Personal mastery is the cultivation of that emotional aspect of learning that so often is neglected in traditional learning settings that focus primarily on the acquisition of information. Senge (1990) gets to the heart of this neglected aspect of curriculum when he states that, for whatever reasons, "we do not pursue emotional development with the same intensity with which we pursue physical and intellectual development. This is all the more unfortunate because full emotional development offers the greatest degree of leverage in attaining our full potential" (p. 143).

Learning communities foster opportunities for students to extend their knowledge into the affective realm of understanding and to realize their own personal dreams or visions. This certainly appears to have been the case with many of the students we observed in our cohort settings. Our students' comments suggest that they experienced a sense of personal mastery through their learning experiences. They spoke of their own personal growth in such phrases as "personal transformation," "self-discoveries," "clarifying and solidifying perceptions," "sharing interpretations," and defining their "internal core."

As professors, we need to be cognizant of the fact that thoughts and ideas often lie hidden within the minds and hearts of our students when we lull them to sleep with our own "inspired lectures." Personal mastery grows out of being actively involved, questioning, and connecting academic content to personal values and self-awareness. Personal mastery provides the seed for visions and for the "covenants" that individuals form with organizations.

Mental Models

Challenging assumptions means questioning the mental models that often constrain our thinking. This dimension of the learning organization encourages members to question current practices, to search for discrepancies that may exist between "what is" and "what ought to be." In learning communities students learn to identify problems and to use the "gap between vision and current reality to generate energy for change" (Senge, 1990, p. 153). This process moves individuals from mere rationality—or forming decisions based on what is known—to intuitive insights. Over 60 years ago, in a 1936 lecture at Princeton University, Chester Barnard (1968b) encouraged leaders to recognize three purposes of thought: to determine truth (a rational process), to determine a course of action (a nonrational or intuitive process), and to persuade others (an intuitive process). The real essence of leadership, he believed, was in the realm of the intuitive. Other writers (Bolman & Deal, 1991; Mintzberg, 1976; Norris & Achilles, 1987) have accented the importance of the intuitive process.

Challenging mental models encourages individuals to examine the underlying assumptions of group expectations and to consider what is right and just for all. Within learning communities students are given opportunities to enter the world of the intuitive through personal reflection, through reflection with others through dialogue, and through clarification of their own values and beliefs.

Shared Values

Conceptualizing a school vision or sense of direction is a shared responsibility based on the shared values of the group. A vision that encompasses not only the vision of the leader, but also the visions of individuals within the group, is a vision that is likely to be pursued. Sergiovanni (1990) speaks of the covenant that individuals share when they unite together through a shared purpose. It is impossible to construct shared visions when individuals are unaware of their personal visions. Dialogue increases individuals' understanding of their own values as well as helping the group find threads of commonality that can sustain members in their group purposes. In our own cohorts, students spoke of this process in the following ways: "Much of what I intuitively knew was made more clear to me," "I learned to define my internal core," and "The group became like an extension of each of us."

Team Learning

Team learning is really learning a new language—a language of discourse. Senge (1990) considers this discourse to be composed of both dialogue and discussion. Dialogue he defines as "a free and creative exploration of complex and subtle issues, a deep 'listening' to one another and suspending of one's own views" (p. 237). It is "a free flow of meaning between people that allows the group to access a larger 'pool of common meaning'" (p. 237).

Dialogue moves collective thought beyond the understanding of one individual to a pool of common meaning that can be constantly developed and changed through repeated dialogue (Norris, Herrmond, & Meisgeier, 1996). Dialogue really teaches individuals *how* to think, for "in dialogue people become observers of their own thinking" (Senge, 1990, p. 242).

Systems Thinking

Not only does team learning increase knowledge and insight, but it also broadens understanding of the holistic thought process. Linear thinkers learn to appreciate the intuitive insights shared by those who think more globally, and intuitive thinkers who delve into the realm of possibilities become more appreciative of the logical structure that others lend to their visions. Through synthesis of talent, the community produces something of real value.

Senge (1990) theorizes that the organization, or total community, begins to think more systemically. Not only do individuals share information across domains, thereby expanding the total knowledge of the organization, but insights and perceptions are shared as well. As these thoughts are connected between members, new insights and knowledge are created that would have remained hidden or unearthed had it not been for the rich dialogue. As a result, the organization begins to think holistically. The rational and intuitive are blended to make new connections and produce greater understandings.

New knowledge and understanding are achieved as individuals share their knowledge and experience with each other. Sharing information promotes new connections and new understandings, which result in the construction of new knowledge. Perspectives are broadened as individuals see beyond the confines of their own classrooms and consider the organization as a whole.

Senge's work helps to confirm the concepts that support our own learning community model. As previously noted, students involved in our learning communities reported an enhanced learning experience through the opportunities they received to share ideas and experiences with one another. They talked of "sharing knowledge," "bringing a piece to the complete puzzle," "exposing their inner thoughts to those in the group," "sharing ideas," "questioning and experimenting in a caring environment," and "learning to value the opinions of others as being important and valid." Dialogue truly strengthens community, for "people actively feel as if they are building something, a new deeper understanding" (Senge, 1990, p. 245). The more individuals practice dialogue, the more they develop a relationship built on a deepening sense of trust—the more they strengthen community.

LOOKING AHEAD

Knowledge is gained both cognitively as well as affectively through dialogue. We turn our attention now to the affective realm and more particularly to the topic of values and philosophy. How are individual and collective values clarified and enhanced through community? What part does values acquisition play in the development of future leaders? These are important questions that we will explore in Chapter 2.

2

Leadership and Community Development Through Values Consciousness

THE HIGHEST FUNCTION of the executive is to develop a deep understanding of himself and his fellows, a knowledge of human nature that includes motivation but reaches beyond it into the domain of value possibilities. Indeed, it could be argued that the very substance of the administrative art form is value (Hodgkinson, 1983).

In Chapter 1, we focused on individual and community development as a reciprocal *process*. In this chapter, we suggest that values, or "concepts of the desirable" (Parsons, 1951, p. 162) form the *substance* of that development. Values shape communities and communities shape values—values, in turn, influence the course of leadership development.

We begin this chapter by investigating the nature of values and the relationship of values to leadership. Next, we present a framework for understanding affective development and connect the growth stages from this framework to our own learning communities. The chapter concludes with a discussion of various theories of values acquisition and their relationship to leadership and community development. As we begin this chapter, it is important first to understand the nature of values, what they are, and how they are acquired.

VALUES AND LEADERSHIP

Values are expressions of personal desires or preferences that give "worth" to particular objects, situations, or conditions (Hodgkinson, 1983). Not only do they signify preferences, but they also reflect an individual's philosophy of the world (Hall & Thompson, 1980) and determine the conscious, or even subconscious, priorities expressed in his/her behavior (Razik & Swanson, 2001). Leadership is, therefore, considered an art form refined through one's knowledge of self as the instrument of that artistry and determined by the values the individual possesses, clarifies, and embodies in his/her behavior (Kouzes & Posner, 1987). Values shape leader and community philosophy and form the notion of *what could be*. Likewise, they determine an individual's aspirations, dreams, and visions—his/her personal dream (Levinson, 1986) or "visualization of self in the world" (Levine, 1989, p. 72). A leader's personal dream establishes direction, serves as a basis for decision making, and provides a source of energy and purpose to his/her life and work. Since values shape personal dreams and visions, they become "the guiding principles of [the leader's life] with respect to personal and social ends [he/she] desire[s] and with respect to moral conduct and personal competence such as honesty and imagination" (Kouzes & Posner, 1993, p. 60).

Values are reflected in the here and now, but they also set the stage for the future—they color possibilities. Values have an impact on shaping the organization in two very important ways. First, leaders' values determine *preservation*. What leaders conserve or leave unchanged demonstrates what they value (Hodgkinson, 1983). For instance, if they hold fast to traditional ways of doing things, and base decisions primarily on past practices, they are inclined to value a more custodial rather than creative orientation to leadership (Norris, 1999).

Second, leaders' values determine the nature of transformation and change (Hodgkinson, 1983). They influence leaders' sense of injustice, the nature of the problems they identify and seek to solve, and the direction that change takes (Hodgkinson, 1983). As an example, leaders who question current practices and envision more humane conditions for those they serve, are energized by the gap between vision and current reality. Senge (1990) refers to this gap as "creative tension" and suggests that it moves leaders from more custodial to more creative practices.

Values, or preferences, are subjective and exist in the inner world of personal feelings rather than in the outer world of reality. Interestingly, though, they have everything to do with shaping that reality (Hodgkinson, 1983). How deeply leaders feel about an issue influences the amount of effort they put forth to fulfill their visions. Likewise, leaders' dedication to an issue depends on how fully integrated their values are. Strength of commitment ultimately determines the degree to which leaders *embody* their values. Leaders embody or "convey their story" by the kind of lives they lead and by the behavior they inspire in others (Gardner, 1995).

Values are espoused, or voiced, and also demonstrated in leaders' actions. Espoused theory suggests what leaders profess to value, while their actual behavior conveys their theories in use (Kottkamp, 1990). Leadership depends on credibility, or congruence between what leaders say and do (Kouzes & Posner, 1993). Credibility, or congruence between espoused values and theory in use, has everything to do with values (Kouzes & Posner, 1993). When a discrepancy exists between what the leader says and does, there is mistrust and the leader is unable to influence the behavior of others. This point is reviewed in great detail through the case studies presented in Chapter 3.

It is without question that leaders do lead from their values, beliefs, and philosophies. The impact of leaders' values is felt, and the quality of that influence depends on the nature of leaders' values, the clarity with which those values are expressed, and the strength of leaders' commitment to those values. What leaders personally value gives form and substance to leadership (Ubben, Hughes, & Norris, 2001).

Clarifying one's values is not a simple task, nor does it ensure that values, once selected, will become permanent choices. Individual values evolve from human personality and experiences; therefore, valuing is a developmental process influenced by the way one views the world and one's place in it. Individuals look to others as they validate their values, and they are influenced in large measure by what others value and inspire. Since values are shaped and further defined through social contact, experiences play an important part in helping individuals clarify and strengthen their values. In that sense, then, communities support and enrich the values of individuals, and individuals support and sustain the values of community.

It is not enough that leaders merely understand their own values. It is crucial that they also appreciate the values of others, since most administrative decisions involve many viewpoints based on varying value perspectives. As leaders interact with organizational members who may have values that differ from theirs, they are faced with difficult choices. They ultimately must decide from among alternative possibilities, based not only on what they personally value, but also on what they perceive to be the needs and values of others. If they have not explored their own values, or are unaware of the values of others, they have little basis for making sound judgments.

Valuing, or the clarification of personal values, is enhanced by personal reflection and by dialogue with others. As discussed in Chapter 1, dialogue differs from mere discussion, for in dialogue community members "suspend assumptions" and enter into a genuine "thinking together . . . allowing the group to discover insights not attainable individually" (Senge, 1990, p. 10). Discussion, on the other hand, merely "heaves ideas back and forth in a winner-takes-all competition" (p. 10). In true learning communities, opportunities exist for genuine dialogue to take place.

Leaders broaden their perspectives and become cognizant of the values of varied stakeholders by being involved in diverse communities where true dialogue takes place (Covrig, 1999). As they continue to expand their personal understanding of collective values, they develop a broader perspective that encourages them to build professional integrity. Leaders are less likely, then, to thoughtlessly comply with every organizational directive. Deeper understanding of varied views fosters thoughtful questioning of current practices in light of human needs. As May (1996) has suggested:

> The person of integrity . . . is responsive to all of the various social groups that have been instrumental in forming his or her "core" self. Contrary to what is sometimes said, professional integrity does not require that people steadfastly stick to the standard commonly recognized for members of a particular profession. (p. 26)

Values form the basis, then, of a transformational style of leadership. Although the organizational structure may greatly inhibit the final fulfillment of the leader's personal dream, as we will discuss at length in Chapter 6, it is the dream itself that provides the inspiration and catalyst to attempt change. Without the dream, little else will happen.

VALUES DEVELOPMENT

There are many theories concerning just how values are developed. We begin our discussion of values development by considering the work of Krathwohl (1964). This author presents a taxonomy of affective development suggesting that values development proceeds through a series of stages that include receiving, responding, valuing, organizing, and characterizing. We discuss these stages with reference to our own students' perceived development, as discussed in Chapter 1.

In the first stage of values development, *receiving*, individuals express a willingness to be receptive to an idea or situation. They develop an initial awareness about something or give it their attention. The initial experience with the idea or situation may cause feelings of uncertainty and discomfort—there is an aspect of unfamiliarity involved. Some students in their reflective journals voiced their feelings related to this developmental stage:

> Our group had a tough time during those first few days.

> The growth of the cohort seemed to be slow as I was experiencing it.

> The atmosphere in the class allowed me to begin to feel secure.

The individual proceeds next to stage two, *responding*, and shows a genuine interest in the situation or idea. A positive change of attitude results in feelings of satisfaction and acceptance of the value. The idea or situation begins to make sense as the individual becomes more comfortable and familiar with it. In journal entries one student expressed a comment that reflects this stage of values development:

> I have been forced to learn about those things toward which I am not naturally inclined, and I have developed an understanding of their importance and the necessity of dealing with them.

In the third stage, *valuing*, the individual accepts the behavior or value and expresses an actual preference or commitment to it. The individual has learned to value the concept. Our students wrote about their own values development in the following ways:

> In contemporary education, teamwork and cooperative groups are big components and if that's what's supposed to be going on in schools and districts, then the university is correct in supporting and modeling that type of system.

> Groupwork enabled us to recognize and utilize each other's strengths, thereby contributing to our growing sense of community.

During the fourth stage, *organizing*, the value is internalized and organized into a value system. From this value system, judgments are formed and responsibility is taken. In journal entries, our students described their own values transitions in the following ways:

> I am amazed how much improved it [the cohort experience compared with traditional program] is. I am committed to do more cooperative learning with my own students.

> I will have a better experience at school this year and I think that others will benefit from the opportunities and ideas that have made better sense to me because of this experience.

Finally, at the highest level of valuing, *characterizing*, values are reflected in the individual's behavior. A set of values is generalized and a philosophy of life is determined. In Chapter 3 we demonstrate this values progression by examining a series of portraitures in which selected students express their values in word and action.

As discussed in Chapter 1, values acquisition is greatly enhanced within a learning community setting when students feel free to explore their values with each other. Such dialogue (Senge, 1990) allows individuals to validate their own beliefs as they openly consider varied viewpoints. In an earlier study discussed in Chapter 1, students talked of their excitement in learning from others' ideas, which seemed to validate and further reinforce their own viewpoints.

As individuals share their experiences with one another through social interchange, they learn to relate in moral and ethical ways. Within the context of community, this is a particularly important concept based heavily on influence. Individuals possess a relatively small number of values, and although certain values may be common to most people, the degree to which those values are held will vary (Hodgkinson, 1983). For this reason, there is a great likelihood that even in diverse groups, bonds of understanding can be formed based on mutually held values. The process of forming these cultural bonds, or shared values, paves the way for true interdependence experienced within community. The students in our cohorts experienced this bonding and in their journals expressed feelings of unity and enhanced friendship as they worked together to accomplish tasks.

Sergiovanni (1992) speaks of this process as "purposing." Through it, community is nourished and individual development is nurtured (Senge, 1990). Community, then, has everything to do with the development of individual and collective values. Exactly how that process takes place will be considered in the following section.

VALUES AND ETHICS

There are differing views among educators concerning the manner in which values and ethics should be included in the formal curriculum (Beck & Murphy, 1997). One approach, a rule-based view, is a rational analysis process that assumes that certain principles of ethical behavior have universal applicability. Based heavily on an ethic of justice (Cohen, 1976; Kohlberg, 1981; Kultgen, 1988; Starratt, 1996; Strike, Haller, & Soltis, 1988), this view of moral development focuses on reciprocity and rights. Those who hold this view see ethics "embodied in rules, ideas, and ideals that transcend individual preferences and can guide objective decision making and problem solving" (Beck & Murphy, 1997, p. 33). The task of the individual, then, is to discover these sound moral principles through logical reasoning.

A second view of ethical development equates ethics with "perspectives that inform perceptions, character, and beliefs" (Beck & Murphy, 1997, p. 33). Advocates of this view believe that ethics are developed through actually living and interacting with others in moral ways (Beck, 1994; Noddings, 1984). Through such interactions, individuals develop an awareness and understanding of others and cultivate ethical ways of viewing situations. This later view of ethical development is experiential. It emanates from an ethic of care that "grounds concepts of the right or the good, not in abstract or impartial rules, but rather in the particular details of specific human situations" (Beck & Murphy, 1997, p. 41). This "cultivation of perspective" fosters the dispositions required for living and working with others in ethical ways. In this sense, "ethics is concerned, not just with reason and action, but also with the development of character" (Beck & Murphy, 1997, p. 41). This approach seems to be aligned with Krathwohl's (1964) notion of values acquisition with the individual moving through the stages of valuing, organizing, and characterizing.

Essentially, this experiential perspective holds that morality is about "being" as well as "doing." Morality is cultivated and developed through the day-to-day interactions and involvement that individuals have with others. Within true learning communities there are continual opportunities to refine one's ethical behavior and to develop a caring attitude that transcends the need for operating merely from a set of "universal principles" that may or may not be appropriate in individual situations. Both of these views have value and a place in educational leadership programs whose aim is to cultivate and develop moral, or transformational, leadership. In either case, there is an emphasis on the need for values development. Just what path this development should take is an area of discussion that will be dealt with in the remainder of this chapter.

VALUES AND LEADERSHIP DEVELOPMENT

Once again, we are reminded of the age-old question: "Are leaders made or born?" We contend that leadership can indeed be developed and that that development takes place effectively within purposefully established settings called learning communities. What is really developed in this process is not just the technical know-how of operating a school or the mere accumulation of a broad knowledge base. What ultimately is developed are the moral and ethical values that will temper the knowledge and skills attained and use them as tools for accomplishing what the leader's spirit and will determine should be valued. That is indeed what Hall and Thompson (1980) suggest when they talk about the *means* for reaching higher levels of values consciousness, which we discuss later in this chapter.

What, then, does leadership development entail? The word *development* suggests a gradual unfolding through a natural process of growth and modification, as suggested by Krathwohl's (1964) taxonomy of affective development. This unfolding takes place in various ways. We view development as a process that evolves incrementally and involves change in form, as well as a process that causes one to reflect upon personal perspectives and behavior in light of what has been learned.

PATHWAYS OF VALUES AND LEADERSHIP DEVELOPMENT

Many theorists have developed models for values or moral development (Gilligan, 1982; Hodgkinson, 1983; Kohlberg, 1981). In this book, we consider two that appear quite similar in orientation, Loevinger's (1976) stage theory and Hall's (1976) theory of values consciousness.

Loevinger's work focuses on ego development, an individual's search for coherence and meaning. The ego, she maintains, is protected as the individual selectively chooses to pay attention only to what fits his or her "ways of knowing and feeling" (Loevinger, 1976, p. 95). These ways of knowing are presented as a series of developmental stages that represent pathways to ego development. Although Loevinger does not divide these developmental stages into categories, there are really two groupings within the stage continuum. Group one depends on *external control* and includes the following stages: (1) Self-Protective, (2) Conformist, and (3) Conscientious-Conformist.

In the Self-Protective Stage, the individual is concerned with controlling situations in order to prevent the discomfort of ambiguity or uncertainty; the main concern is maintaining safety. The individual at this stage is not opposed to being controlled by others, for that ensures that his or her safety will be the concern of others in charge. In stage two, the Conformist Stage, there is a tendency to conform to the desires and policies outlined by others, in order to maintain that sense of security. The person becomes preoccupied with compliance with institutional rules and there is a desire for acceptance and approval. In the third stage, the Conscientious-Conformist Stage, the individual moves toward an increased awareness of self and is more aware of his/her own feelings. During this phase, there is less conformity to the rules and more individual expression.

However, since the person at this stage has not fully developed confidence in self, there is still a tendency to slip back into a more conforming stage during times of stress. In all stages in the first grouping, the individual is dependent on external controls such as structure, rules, and established procedures to ensure that there is stability in life and that he or she is afforded the security not yet internally developed.

In Loevinger's (1976) second grouping, the individual has gained an *internal sense* of security that enables self-reliance. The stages within this grouping include: (1) Conscientious Stage, (2) Individualistic Stage, and (3) Integrated Stage. In the Conscientious Stage, the individual develops increased awareness of others and sensitivity to personal feelings and choices. There is a desire to live up to high ideals and to be self-critical and reflective. As the individual gains greater self-knowledge, tolerance for self and others increases along with recognition that individual differences are indeed a strength—qualities that are reflected in the Individualistic Stage. This awareness, then, leads to deepening personal relationships. Finally, in the Integrated Stage, individuals gain self-acceptance and understand their own realities. This leads to self-respect and a deepening understanding of self and others.

Loevinger (1976) points out that the ego has a natural resistance to change that reinforces the need for social interaction with peers as a means for developing values consciousness. A quick review of the learning communities model that we introduced in Chapter 1 suggests a similar progression of individual development based on the interaction, purpose, and interdependence afforded through community. Table 2.1 outlines that progression in comparison to Loevinger's stages. As Table 2.1 suggests, there is similarity between the learning community model indicators of security and support and the external control stages of Loevinger's

Table 2.1. Comparison of Loevinger's Stage Theory with Levels of Individual Development Within Learning Communities

Loevinger's Stages	Learning Communities
Self-protective	
Conformist	Support
Conscientious-Conformist	Security
Conscientious	Friendship
Individualistic	Knowledge acquisition
Integrated	Personal dream

model. Similarly, the friendship, knowledge, and personal dream stages of the learning community model correspond to the internal control stages of Loevinger's model. Both models seem to suggest a similar progression.

Hall and Thompson (1980) also consider values development to be a developmental process that proceeds in a sequential manner according to a hierarchy of values goals. They emphasize, however, that the attainment of a particular values consciousness phase is mediated by two important variables: the *means*, or skills necessary for actualizing the value, and the *values goal* desired. In other words, individuals cannot appreciate, or become aware of, a higher-level value (or goal) until they have the actual skills (or means) to accomplish that values goal. This is where it is important to consider the content that is acquired within learning community settings—the knowledge and performance skills that enable means—as well as the social context in which values, or dispositions, are acquired. In order for optimum values consciousness to occur, it is important that purposeful attention be given to the integration of knowledge, skills, and dispositions as means for reaching higher levels of values awareness. This perspective on developing values consciousness has major implications for those who prepare future school leaders. It suggests that within the learning context, there should be opportunities not only for the concepts and skills of transformational leadership to be taught, but also for students to practice their learned skills through the process of living and working together in community.

CYCLES OF GROWTH

As previously noted, Hall (1976) considers values acquisition to be a developmental process that proceeds through distinct cycles of growth. He separates his developmental cycles into two groups comparable to those of Loevinger. Hall's model, as well as Loevinger's, supports the learning community model previously presented. Table 2.2 compares Loevinger's and Hall's models.

Hall's first group represents a view of leadership and followership based on authority or external control. The cycles of growth in this group include (1) the *Primal Cycle*, characterized by security, self-interest, and physical survival, (2) the *Familial Cycle*, symbolized by the family as protector and legitimate authority, and (3) the *Institutional Cycle*, focused on adherence to legitimate authority symbolized in institutions. As with Loevinger's group one categories, authority originates outside the self. The individual is compliant as a follower, and as a leader places high priority on external control mechanisms that treat followers in a subjective

Table 2.2. Comparison of Loevinger's Stage Theory with Hall's Theory of Values Consciousness

Loevinger's Stages	*Hall's Cycles of Values Growth*
Group One	
Self-Protective	Primal
Conformist	Familial
Conscientious-Conformist	Institutional
Group Two	
Conscientious	Interpersonal
Individualistic	Communal/Collaborative
Integrated	Mystical

manner. As reflected in Table 2.2, these cycles are strikingly similar to the stages in Loevinger's first grouping: *Self-Protective*, *Conformist*, and *Conscientious-Conformist*.

In Hall's (1976) second group of growth cycles, authority originates within the individual. Intrinsic control and motivation become the mechanisms through which one leads and follows. Reflected in that group are (1) the *Interpersonal Cycle*, focused on the self and individual values as the basis of interpretation, (2) the *Communal/Collaborative Cycle*, defined by clear personal values emphasizing humanistic concerns, and (3) the *Mystical Cycle*, characterized by individual integration, self-actualization, and justice.

As suggested by Hall (1976), these cycles move progressively from the Primal Cycle, which focuses on self and basic survival, to the Mystical Cycle, which offers a broader life view. The Mystical Cycle embraces self and others as the individual moves beyond mere self-interests and organizational concerns to awareness and responsive interest in a global community of human beings. Loevinger's second group, the *Conscientious*, *Individualistic*, and *Integrated* developmental stages, is very similar to Hall's second grouping. Both reinforce the basic premise of an ethic of care, a concept we will discuss further in Chapter 4. Both center the individual's values solidly in the realm of community.

PHASES OF CONSCIOUSNESS

Hall has reconfigured the six developmental cycles into four phases of consciousness, as shown in Table 2.3, suggesting that movement from

Table 2.3. Hall's Theory of Values Consciousness: Cycles of Growth Related to Phases of Consciousness

Cycles of Growth	Phases of Consciousness
Primal	Phase One
Familial	
Institutional	Phase Two
Interpersonal	Phase Three
Communal/Collaborative	
Mystical	Phase Four

one phase to the next requires an individual to become conscious (aware) of that phase by (1) understanding the world from that perspective, (2) perceiving oneself as functioning within that world, or (3) having desired human needs satisfied within that phase.

A phase of values consciousness is governed not only by the goals or needs the individual seeks to satisfy within that phase, but by the means, or skills, required to fulfill the goals of that values phase. In other words, before an individual can truly reach the next highest goal on the values continuum, he or she must possess the necessary skills, or means, for attaining that goal. This evolution was demonstrated by some of our students who entered the learning community with feelings of insecurity when they started interacting with others. As they developed skills in interpersonal relationships, they began to aspire toward a higher values goal of belonging. This same evolution has major implications for leadership development and for shaping organizational context. Leaders will lead only to a phase of consciousness level for which they possess the skills that enable that level of values awareness to emerge. Interestingly, as individuals collect to form organizations, an organizational context will reflect the phase of values consciousness of its members (Morgan, 1986) and will be elevated as those individuals are given the skills, or means, to fulfill higher-level goals.

Therefore, it becomes the leader's role to provide conditions that will foster the development of those means and thereby enable the group to reach higher phases of values consciousness. This fact has major implications for those who desire to enhance students' leadership development through learning communities.

With each step in the growth process, the individual becomes more inclusive, receptive, and global. Each phase of values awareness, or growth, is marked by a style of leadership that progresses from a more directive to a more collaborative orientation. Based on Hall's theory, the individual's view of life shapes the direction of his or her leadership. Phases of development and their resulting leadership cycles are mediated by the instrumental skills necessary to support them, a concept that we will address in Chapter 5. In the portraitures we present in Chapter 3, we have attempted to classify the values expressed by former students (now practicing school administrators) into the cycle of values development that their words, and the expressed perceptions of their staff, seemed to indicate.

Hall's Theory in Combination with Morgan's Metaphors

In expanding Hall's theory one step further and exploring the four phases in which the values stages are depicted, it is helpful to also consider the notion of organizational metaphor as a lens for exploring organizational context in relation to these leadership phases. Morgan (1986) distinguishes seven metaphors of organizational context. We consider several of these metaphors as frames for interpreting Hall's four phases of consciousness (see Table 2.4). First, however, it is important to understand the concept of "metaphor" as it applies to organizational context.

Morgan defines an organizational metaphor as "*a way of thinking* and *a way of seeing* that pervade how we understand our world generally" (Morgan, 1986, p. 12). He suggests that, although organizations are "complex and paradoxical phenomena that can be understood in many different

Table 2.4. Hall's Theory of Values Consciousness Compared with Morgan's Images of Organizations

Morgan's Images of Organizations	Hall's Theory of Values Consciousness	
	Cycles of Growth	*Phases of Consciousness*
Machines	Primal	Phase One
	Familial	
Organisms	Institutional	Phase Two
	Interpersonal	Phase Three
	Communal/collaborative	
Brains	Mystical	Phase Four

ways" (p. 13), the metaphor enables one to highlight a certain interpretation of the organizational context. In the following section, these metaphors represent interpretations that might be held by leaders coming from the different phases of values consciousness introduced by Hall. Again, these phases are portrayed in Table 2.4 in comparison to the metaphors of organizations.

The Four Phases Compared with Organizational Metaphors

Individuals at *Phase One* are consumed with their own self-interest and have little empathy for others. Since the major emphasis is survival, they are highly motivated to remain safe and to preserve things in a stable, secure manner. There is a great need at this phase to ensure that life is predictable and that it conforms to known patterns. This is particularly true during periods of increased stress or uncertainty, when there is enhanced need for self-preservation and less tolerance for ambiguity. Since structure, predictability, and control give the illusion of "safety," leaders who operate from this phase of values consciousness seek safety in the tried and true. The machine metaphor (Morgan, 1986) best exemplifies their mode of operation.

When schools are viewed as machines, they exhibit qualities of efficiency, predictability, and order. The organization's daily operation is highly structured and operates as a closed system—organizational members are unaware of, or unresponsive to, the changing needs of the school's internal and external environments. These schools are policy-driven settings characterized by a bureaucratic hierarchy that tends to stifle the initiative and creativity of organizational members (Argyris, 1957). Leaders attempt to control both power and knowledge, and manage the school and its people so that order, predictability, and tradition are maintained. On the surface, all appears balanced and smooth running; however, decay can easily occur in such stagnant environments. These schools face real danger of becoming outdated and obsolete. When schools are designed as machines, leaders tend to manage rather than lead, for there is comfort in stability.

In *Phase Two* the need for social interaction becomes prevalent as the individual reaches beyond his or her need for self-preservation to appreciate the needs of others. There is an increasing desire to belong—not only within family and social groups, but also to organizations. Organizational affiliation is still seen as strict adherence to rules, policies, and procedures since leaders at this phase strive to operate "by the book." At the same time, they project a caring, considerate attitude toward subordinates, more in keeping with the organism metaphor (Morgan, 1986). Since schools are viewed as "families," there is emphasis on collegiality and on instilling a sense of belonging among the staff. Often there is conflict between these two desires, and the individual experiences some discomfort in trying to manage both task and relationship. This stage forms a bridge between the machine and organism metaphors. Neither metaphor is dominant.

During *Phase Three*, individuality emerges as a creative response to life takes the place of institutional conformity. Individuals emerge as "their own persons" with increased motivation for self-actualization and a genuine empathy and deep respect for human life. Leaders at this phase of values consciousness find the organism metaphor a compatible view of school context for it emphasizes the uniqueness of individuals and the need for their continued development.

The organism metaphor reflects growth and adaptation. Centered on interdependence and collaboration, these educational settings emphasize individuality, uniqueness, and self-renewal. They are responsive, open organizations that meet the changing needs of their internal and external environments. In such schools, leaders serve as facilitators of a shared mission that unites organizational members through purposeful commitment. Standardization of method is far less important than the results achieved or the impact realized. Human needs are acknowledged and met while growth is facilitated.

Finally, in *Phase Four*, individuals begin to operate from a more global, systemic perspective. There is an increased desire for harmony, community, and integration of values, beliefs, and ideas. Leaders view the world beyond the borders of the school with a deepening appreciation for the larger community and for societal issues. Principals take on a proactive stance by becoming more involved in the critical questioning of current practice. There is a transformational aspect to leadership that seeks to make a difference in education and in the lives of others, as well as a strong desire to build community.

Schools guided by this phase of values consciousness reflect the brain metaphor. They are learning communities characterized by thinking and learning perspectives that emphasize reflective problem finding aimed toward improvement of current practice. The image of these schools is holistic, with both the rational and intuitive dimensions of leadership highly evidenced. Knowledge, as well as power, is widely dispersed throughout the organization. Distributed power and knowledge enable adaptation to occur and new designs and approaches to be generated. These schools are characterized by a true sense of community; knowledge is not only shared and stored, but is generated. Leaders are facilitators who enable the free flow of communication and exchange of ideas. They are also people developers who set forth conditions that foster the empowerment of others.

SUMMARY

The context of a school is indicative of the preferences, values, and habits of the individuals that the school comprises. Out of these contextual frames, leadership not only emerges but also becomes influential in shaping the future directions of the organization. There is a direct relationship between the evolution of organizational contexts and the leadership orientations that provide the seeds for their development. The highest level of values attainment embraces unity and celebrates an organizational brain metaphor (Morgan, 1986) that emphasizes shared responsibility and the common good.

Through personal reflection, leaders encounter their beliefs, strengthen their convictions, and challenge their thinking toward higher levels of moral commitment. Self-awareness initiates this developmental journey that begins with values awareness, leads to aspiration, and eventually becomes action. Each step in the development of values consciousness provides a deeper understanding of one's moral responsibility to others and results in leadership that inspires others to be responsive to human needs. Leaders and followers mutually influence each other to embrace higher phases of values consciousness (Burns, 1978). As these higher levels of values consciousness are realized, leadership does, indeed, become a transformational process.

LOOKING AHEAD

Within each of the learning communities we are striving to achieve in our leadership preparation programs, we have provided students opportunities to take part in the clarification of their values, to discuss values-related issues through genuine dialogue (Senge, 1990), and to express their values through reflective journals, platforms, and portfolios—activities that we discuss in more detail in Chapter 5. In Chapter 3, we share the portraitures of four selected students—one representing each of our university programs. As you explore their stories, you will encounter their espoused values, expressed during and after their formal leadership training. You also will observe their theories in action as practicing school administrators, based on the impressions gleaned from individuals within their respective schools. We conclude the chapter by analyzing their portraitures in relation to their attained levels of values consciousness as outlined by Hall (1976) and their preferred images of a school's context based on the work of Morgan (1986).

Our intent in sharing these portraitures is not to suggest that our learning communities determined the nature of their values, but rather to demonstrate that the experiences provided them opportunities to express and clarify those values. These portraitures attempt to show, then, how the individuals' expressed values, once clarified, are embodied in their leadership.

3

Principals as Developing Leaders

GIVEN OUR DISPOSITION to believe that there are various levels of leadership values and that those matter to a leader's work, we also think that what leaders do, and encourage others to do, needs to be consistent with the values they espouse and demonstrate through action. If espoused values constitute what they believe, and their theory in use represents demonstration of those beliefs (Kottkamp, 1982), congruence between belief and action is observed and credibility as a leader develops (Kouzes & Posner, 1993). Discrepancies are quickly noted by followers, and the trust a leader is attempting to build is thwarted. Indeed, the leader may experience serious difficulty in trying to influence the behavior of others if he or she is found to be inconsistent in values and actions. Examples abound of leaders, principals particularly, who try to promote a particular directive but who do not believe in its efficacy. Faculty quickly see the discrepancy; district leaders pressure the principal to abide by the directive; the principal often cannot regain the trust of either side.

If values clarification in the preparation of school leaders is important to their success on the job, students of leadership need to begin thinking about their own levels of values consciousness and their beliefs about organizations. A way to guide such development is to encourage reflection in leader preparation programs. Through self-assessment instruments, reflective writings, regular feedback from the professor and colleagues, and, most important of all, the educational platform, students can come to a clearer understanding of themselves as future educational leaders.

Sergiovanni and Starratt (1979) presented the idea of the educational platform as the way school leaders develop their assumptions or beliefs that "deal with the way children and youth grow, with the purposes of schooling, with the nature of learning, with pedagogy or teaching, with educational programs, and with school climate" (p. 214). Because "educators make practical decisions about practice based upon convictions, assumptions, and attitudes" (Sergiovanni & Starratt, 1993, p. 142) and because educators can begin to assess their own internal consistency by writing and discussing their beliefs, the platform can become a significant part of the educational experience of future leaders. As faculty members in four institutions of higher education, we chose to incorporate platforms in our teaching. As researchers, we were interested in whether there might be long-term value in platform development. While several major ingredients that should be included in any educational platform are proposed in the literature, we looked specifically at four key elements in which our students, and later leaders, discussed their views of educational leadership: the purpose of education, the role of the administrator, the role of the teacher, and the role of the student.

Since reflective writing simply provides espoused values, we decided to follow four students as they became school leaders and to evaluate whether they were indeed practicing what they said they believed. Three questions guided our work: (1) Does the leadership behavior of former members of a graduate cohort—now practicing school administrators— reflect the values they espoused during their administrative preparation programs? (2) Does their behavior suggest that they have reached a level of values consciousness compatible with transformational leadership? (3) Have they transferred their espoused views and enhanced dispositions to the workplace?

We began with values that students articulated through platform development and other reflective writings, and compared them with values the students later expressed in personal interviews. The expressed values, from both time periods, were then compared with the students' theories in use as perceived by their teachers. The espoused values and theories in use were then analyzed using Hall's Phases of Values Consciousness (Hall, Kalven, Rosen, & Taylor, 1991) and Morgan's (1986) metaphors of organizational context (i.e., machines, organisms, and brains), as described in Chapter 2. A portraiture was then developed for each student based on the written documents, participant and staff interviews, and the analysis.

This chapter briefly describes the students' experiences in their leadership preparation programs and presents the four portraitures and an analysis of each leader's espoused theory versus theory in use. A comparative analysis of the four portraitures provides information regarding predominant themes discovered across cases. Conclusions are suggested as to students' transfer of espoused leadership values to the work setting, along with programmatic suggestions for practice. These portraitures were adapted from an earlier study by the authors (Norris, Basom, Yerkes, & Barnett, 1996) and are presented as a means of illustrating leaders' development as a reflection of their values and movement toward transformational leadership.

STUDENTS' EXPERIENCE IN ADMINISTRATOR PREPARATION PROGRAMS

During their graduate experiences, students in each of the university cohorts kept reflective journals, developed educational platforms, and took part in personality and leadership assessments designed to enhance self-awareness and insight regarding their future leadership potential. (Chapter 5 provides a detailed discussion of curricular foundations and instructional techniques, and Chapter 6 discusses transfer of learning.) This self-knowledge formed a backdrop for internalizing course content and field-based application of learning. Students applied their knowledge in group problem-solving activities within their respective educational settings. Thus, not only did they study about leadership, but they related leadership theories to their own lives and personalities and applied leadership concepts in actual group problem-solving activities. An integrated learning approach provided a strong basis for conceptualizing their personal views, or espoused theories, of leadership.

Students in the four programs were asked to develop educational platforms based on their learning experiences. In addition to the platform, reflective journals were kept in various classes throughout these students' programs. In them students were asked regularly to consider their readings, field-based activities, writing, and personal and professional development. Faculty provided feedback and reflective questions to assist students in their development. Assessments also were given to students, as a way to help them consider their strengths, capabilities, and interests. While the particular instruments varied from program to program, all students participated in self-assessment with feedback from professors and the cohort.

Thus, while each of the four graduate programs, all influenced to some degree by the faculty's participation in the Danforth Principal Preparation Program and network, differed somewhat from the others, certain instructional strategies were constant: the cohort, the platform, regular student reflection on work, a voice in their activities, and the development of interpersonal relationships through cohort-building activities.

THE LEADERS

The four leaders were students in previous cohort programs at the Universities of Houston, Wyoming, and Northern Colorado, and California State

University, Fresno. They shared their platforms and their dreams with their instructors and their cohorts. Later, these leaders were willing to discuss the successes and occasional disappointments they experienced as school leaders. Their staffs, who told the truth as they saw it, told us about their leaders.

Amy Smithfield

Amy wrote in her journal that she is guided by Cicero's aphorism: *Vivere est cogitare* (to think is to live). She also noted that "if a student is taught that learning is contagious, one idea will spark another." Amy epitomized that "spark." From her beginning days as a member of a cohort at the University of Houston, to her current work as a school leader, one gains the impression that there is something in this individual that is far above the "ordinary," a sense of commitment and enthusiasm that ignites others to follow and "want to become."

Espoused Theory: As a Student. Assessments completed during Amy's graduate days describe her as imaginative, creative, intuitive, and having such strengths as an "imaginative ability," "understanding of people," and ability to "recognize problems."

These qualities were clearly expressed in Amy's educational platform. As she indicated, "We, as educators, will attack the challenges of society by arming [future citizens/leaders] with the courage and skill to create—no matter what the occupation." Likewise, she saw the role of the principal as "service to others," and "the initiator of boundless educational opportunities."

Amy recognized the place of leadership in the improvement of societal conditions and viewed the leader as one who could "bridge the gap of relating social concerns to operational matters."

Espoused Theory: As a Leader. In 1990, Amy became an assistant principal. She was one of the first African American female school administrators in a previously Caucasian, affluent, Houston area school district known for its forward thinking and commitment to quality education. In 1993, she was selected by her peers as the Outstanding Assistant Principal in the Houston area and honored by the Texas Association of Secondary School Principals.

Amy's school was "north of the freeway," an area that is viewed by many as "less desirable." The middle school of 875 students is 75% Hispanic and 15% African American. It is characterized by a high concentration of low socioeconomic students, over 50% coming from single-parent homes.

In an earlier platform, Amy had written these words: "I will concern myself with reaching the total child—but recognition [of the child's needs] is simply not enough. Acknowledgment extends its arms beyond the complacent boundaries of mere recognition and helps to foster in each child a sense of belonging to a greater community, thus solidifying the need for an education."

Amy became committed to seeing that the children in the neighborhood were provided their just due. "I worked a lot with parents and students on the attitudes of inferiority." I stressed with them that "just because your school is 'north of the freeway,' doesn't mean that you can't have what you need. You can have it; you need to ask for it. . . . You can have it right now."

Amy believes that the job of the educator is to instill a desire for learning and to nurture the learner. She is adamant that learning is a continual process that does not take place just within the school. She insists that "we need to take children out into the environment . . . have them involved in problem solving . . . constantly strive to better their perspectives of their world. It can't just be formal education! We learn from the kids, too! They need to see that there is reciprocity there!"

Respect for human life seems to undergird all that Amy believes in: "We are here to support one another . . . all the lives that we touch." She talks of community, connectedness—that sense of a "circle" where individuals are viewed as equal contributors to a greater purpose. "Seeking out the advice of many in working through solutions" as well as "building connections with others . . . building meaning" are important concepts voiced by Amy.

Amy believes that being a leader is "being a role model." Constantly aware of her own need to "become all that [she] can be and share it with others," she feels a need to constantly challenge herself. "I don't like it," she states, "when I see myself making mistakes. I need to stop and question, 'Is what I am doing really important?' . . . It takes someone to verbally challenge me at times. I need to interact with those outside of education; they are the ones that are most questioning. They challenge my thinking."

Amy is quiet, almost humble, in response to questions about the honors she has received. Being selected as an outstanding leader and serving as president of the Houston Area Middle School Association seem secondary to the intrinsic rewards she receives from working with others. "My personal pleasures come from what I have done to help students become 'sparked.' When they come back to school later and tell me, it makes me feel good." The positive remarks she receives when parents and teachers express their appreciation are equally rewarding.

Theory in Use: Teachers' Perceptions. At the time of the teacher interviews, Amy was no longer a physical presence in the school where she had been an assistant principal for 7 years. It soon became apparent to this interviewer, however, that "the spark" of Amy's influence was still very much in evidence.

Teachers talked of Amy and her work with obvious regard. They appreciated the sense of integrity that Amy displayed and the deep respect for humankind that they saw permeating her behavior. As one teacher remarked, "She held teachers in the highest esteem. I always felt respected, complimented by her. It was a genuine pleasure to work with her. The highest regard came from her to me."

Amy's acknowledgment of others extended to students as well. One teacher remarked that "her supportiveness was astounding. . . . She had a profound understanding of the emotional needs of children . . . great compassion . . . support." However, one teacher remarked that perhaps, at times, Amy "could have been more affirming to teachers."

Amy's theory in use, as perceived by her teachers, is clearly evident. Teachers perceived that Amy saw the purpose of education as total development of the student—emotionally and socially. They felt that she promoted the idea of "children learning to learn . . . learning to guide themselves." As one teacher remarked, "I've seen few administrators who could deal with so many different types of children; she wanted to bring every child to their full potential."

Teachers viewed Amy as an instructional leader. They knew that Amy felt all teachers were accountable for each child's learning and "responsible for designing a healthy atmosphere so that every child could succeed." As one teacher suggested, "She encouraged us to become knowledgeable of the student. She wanted us to know more about each child's background to make connections between the child's learning needs and the content to be taught." Professionalism was important to Amy; teachers viewed her as modeling professional behavior and knew that she "expected it from all teachers." They saw her as a "calming and inspiring influence." As one teacher expressed, "She was right there with us, always; never that separated."

Teachers we interviewed recognized that Amy had high expectations for each child and wanted students to "strive to maximize their own potential." It was important to Amy, they believed, for "kids to work to the best of their abilities, but in a healthy way." They knew that she "wanted learning to be a joyful experience" for all students and thought students "should see their lives as fulfilling."

As an administrator, Amy was viewed as having "good people skills;

she didn't try to take over." Teachers seemed to agree that she was "responsive, honest," and "always going that little bit extra that makes a difference."

Teachers described Amy as "inspiring," "ready to share ideas," "invigorating." As one teacher remarked, "I saw her as a broadening influence. . . . She wanted us to look beyond where we currently were to a more complete view." Most agreed that Amy was always ready to acknowledge others' potential and to foster their development. "She encouraged me to go to grad school," "to interview teachers," "to join organizations," were some of the comments heard from teachers. Most seemed to agree that Amy "kept abreast of new theories and wanted [teachers] to apply new knowledge to situations."

One teacher stated that she was "surprised at what Amy could accomplish . . . the details! All seemed geared to making teachers feel important!" Still another recounted, "She demonstrated intelligence, smoothness. . . . She could put it [leadership] on like a coat!" The words "gaiety" and "humor" seemed to round out the impressions teachers had of this leader. They saw her as a principled individual whose "vision for the organization was that of a family: concerned adults; children who felt that concern; and teachers who provided support."

Case Perspective. The consistency between espoused theory and theory in use is clearly evident in the above portraiture. Table 3.1 illustrates the consistency in Amy's espoused theory and her theory in use. Noteworthy, also, is the phase of values consciousness that Amy's behavior and values seem to indicate. She is on her way to becoming a transformational leader with her central values of service, growth and development for self and others, and desire to make society a better place.

Amy has come to a turning point in her life. After 7 years as an assistant principal, she has decided to leave. She has become an administrative intern in the Department of Personnel, where she finds that she is continuing to be motivated by service to others. "How can I help to make the best connections [in selection/placement] for the good of the kids?" she asks.

Moving on in her career was not an easy decision. "I could do the job, but I needed to make more of a difference. I needed the spark to keep going!" She admits that there are adjustments she must make. "I have been viewed as a leader. Now I've got to prove myself again . . . have someone check my work. I'm the same person I have always been; the title is just different!" Her sense of confidence and inner strength should ease her transition.

One feels a sense of inspiration in talking with Amy and in knowing

Table 3.1. Analysis of Leadership Values Espoused and Reflected in Leadership Behavior: Amy

Motto	Terms/Phrases Espoused	Behaviors Noted by Faculty	Organizational Metaphor	Growth Cycle and Values Consciousness Stage
Vivere est cogitare (to think is to live)	Service	Integrity	Brain	Communal/Collaborative Cycle:
	Supporter, catalyst	Respect for humankind	Interdependence	Clear personal values that emphasize humanistic concerns
	Stimulator, nurturer	Understanding of emotional needs	Empowerment	
	Continual learning	Designer of healthy atmosphere	Thinking, learning, organization	
	Connections, interdependent	Calming and aspiring influence	Collaborating	Phase Four Values Consciousness:
	Community	Served, participated equally	Holistic	Global, systemic perspective; desire for harmony, community, and the integration of values, beliefs, and ideas
	Change, initiation, renewal	Fostered others equally	Evolving, dynamic	
	Shared knowledge	Acknowledged potential		
	Contributions			
	Empowerment			

that no matter what role she fulfills in the educational arena, those influenced by her leadership will be the benefactors. She will continually question the relevance of her life and the contributions she is making. The "spark" is there and will remain.

Brad Norman

A quote from a Nike commercial, "The race goes not to the swift but to those who realize that there is no finish line," exemplified Brad Norman's belief in being a lifelong learner as he entered the Snowy Range Cohort at the University of Wyoming in the summer of 1993. Brad wrote in his reflective journal that his childhood did not offer many models for lifelong learning but that he always dreamed and believed his dreams could become reality. "Every kid should be able to sit on the swing set at night and dream like I did. Every kid should have his dreams come true like I did."

Brad was still a dreamer as he prepared for a future leadership role. On that first summer in his doctoral program, Brad's dreams included that of being a principal at a school "where every teacher wants to teach, every parent wants to send his/her child, and where every kid wants to go to school."

Espoused Theory: As a Student. Personal growth was the core of Brad's personal platform. Growing personally was what allowed Brad to grow professionally. As he examined his life roles, he used the adage that "there is no finish line [or] yardstick for each of those roles." As spouse, father, son, and educator, Brad often returned to a quote from John Kennedy to inspire him. "History is a relentless master. It has no present, only the past rushing into the future. To try and hold fast is to be swept aside." He understood that by trying to "hold fast" he would not be serving any of his roles faithfully. He continually searched for new ways of growing and of helping others do the same, and believed that being a principled leader should be the focus of all his life roles.

Brad's educational background includes work as a special education teacher, coach, assistant principal of a large junior high school, and elementary principal. These experiences provided a basis for much of the reflective activity that helped to shape his espoused beliefs.

Espoused Theory: As a Leader. Brad became principal of Dutot High School in 1995, a school of 1,350 students, mostly Caucasian, with a 10% minority population of African American and Hispanic students. The school has a special education population of over 10% and houses a branch of the Wyoming School for the Deaf. In the past year, Dutot High School has produced five merit scholar finalists and offers a wide variety of activities and academic programs. The school is the recipient of bond money that has afforded it with Internet capabilities in almost all classrooms. The community has supported the school in landscaping and wiring for Internet access. The school also houses a day care center, funded by the school district, for the infants of school-aged mothers.

As its leader, Brad has a personal vision of a school "where every kid can come and get what is needed in the realm of academics and in the areas of emotional support in order to grow and develop into a happy person." Brad is also very concerned about the issue of equity. He does not want a school that does good things for the "rich kid" or the "at-risk kid," but rather one in which all students who enter find the opportunities they need.

Brad does not believe in top-down administration but believes that schools should be driven "by the people," who include teachers, parents, students, staff, and community members. He views the organization as a living organism based on interdependence of faculty, adaptability to change, and productivity through people. He believes that teachers at Dutot feel empowered to make decisions that contribute to the growth of the school.

Theory in Use: Teachers' Perceptions. Staff members and faculty described what they perceive to be the underlying principles that guide Brad Norman as a school leader: what Brad stands for, what he articulates as the purpose of education, and what he expects from students and staff. The most important thing for Brad, people agreed, is for students to be provided with an education that prepares all kids for future endeavors, to help them grow not only academically but in all ways. Clearly the "all" is very important to Brad. As one teacher stated, "His philosophy is that he wants to touch all kids somehow and make sure that each one of them has a positive experience . . . and in all areas as much as possible." Brad is a "students' principal; he's always in the halls making them [the students] feel good."

To accomplish Brad's educational goal, the faculty feel that he expects them to ensure that all students have a "positive experience" at Dutot High; that all kids "feel good about coming to school." Brad views the faculty as the front line. It is what faculty do in the classroom that's important to achieving the educational goals of the school. It's their job "to build those connections, to make sure the students feel good about coming to school," to be mentors and guides, to create the spark for each student. "I think he feels that we have the most important job in the school and that he's here to support us in any way that he can to make sure we get our job done."

Teachers are in agreement that they form a close-knit group, most of whom work together as a team. They agree that there are still some pockets of resistance to change, but they don't see that as unusual in an organization the size of Dutot High. Developing a team spirit is not easy, but teachers believe Brad is making headway; things are definitely on the upswing. There appears to be more of an overall school spirit since Brad's arrival, more excitement, "and I think it's because of Brad, people rally around him; he causes teachers to get fired up." Since Brad and his assistant principals appear to have fun at their jobs, faculty get excited about coming to work. Brad is seen as a cheerleader, not only for kids, but also for faculty and staff. "He has taken what was good [about Dutot High] and made it better." This researcher noted that the faculty room is a pleasant place to visit with colleagues. Teachers were upbeat, humor was evident, popcorn was plentiful, and it was apparent that teachers enjoyed working in that environment.

Teachers believe that they have the ability to make decisions related to better serving kids in their classrooms. "We are in charge of our classroom," was a commonly heard theme. Teachers feel in total control when it comes to making decisions that affect how and what they teach. Because of Brad's openness, and his willingness to listen, all faculty sense they are able to have input into all school business. Because they feel no fear of retribution, teachers often find themselves offering advice on any or all parts of the school operation. Brad likes to get teachers together to discuss ideas and issues. He encourages examining various options on most issues but doesn't try to impose his thinking on the group. "He's really good at getting adverse groups of people together, having them set a goal and setting them on the right track. He isn't one to say, 'This is our focus'; he wants us to come up with that."

Case Perspective. Brad's espoused theory seems quite consistent with his theory in use as perceived by his staff. Table 3.2 shows his emphasis on growth and self-actualization for self and others. Brad is a developer of people who places high regard on the contributions of others. This tendency is reflective of the organistic metaphor and places Brad in the Interpersonal Cycle of growth and phase three of values consciousness.

After only one year in his position, Brad appears to have established considerable credibility with those who work beside him. He is determined to continue to pursue that dream, so vivid during his graduate school days, of being a principled leader. He does not feel that he has "arrived"; there is still much to be accomplished.

Table 3.2. Analysis of Leadership Values Espoused and Reflected in Leadership Behavior: Brad

Motto	Terms/Phrases Espoused	Behaviors Noted by Faculty	Organizational Metaphor	Growth Cycle and Values Consciousness Stage
"The race goes not to the swift but to those who realize there is no finish line."	Lifelong learning Personal growth Continual self-renewal Equity of opportunity Academic and emotional growth	Provides students with opportunities to prepare for future endeavors Touches all students; provides growth experiences Fosters positive climate and motivation Mentors and guides	<u>Organism</u> Growth Responsiveness Adaptability	<u>Interpersonal Cycle:</u> Focus on personal and group values as the basis for action <u>Phase Three Values Consciousness:</u> Individuality takes the place of institutional conformity; respect for the dignity and worth of others; desire for continuous development for self and others

Brad believes, as Andrew Jackson did, that "one man with courage makes a majority." Leaders must be able to inspire and motivate followers into action. Brad states that principled leaders of today "charge many private hills on a daily basis," and that without a core set of beliefs and a sense of personal vision, it is difficult for a leader to serve effectively as a steward to the people served. Brad seems to understand that the world will continue to change, and he is determined to be a player: "I hope that by always moving toward, but never crossing, my finish line, I will continue to grow throughout my life. My role as a leader and professional will change, but I believe the values and beliefs I hold in my heart are untouchable. Time will be the judge of that."

Ross Williams

Ross Williams believes that "education is the golden ticket . . . it is an investment in human capital. What better way to invest in our future than by investing in our youth."

Ross Williams entered California State University, Fresno, in 1993, with a background in counseling, teaching, and school administration. While he was earning an administrative credential, he participated in various reflective sessions with his cohort, developed a professional port-folio and platform, and kept a fieldwork journal. These experiences, he believes, were instrumental in helping to shape his theory of leadership.

Espoused Theory: As a Student. Ross clearly articulated a vision of school-ing and educational leadership built on the value of people and relation-ships. His vision contained a strong sense of responsibility for preparing young people for the future and for their place in our democracy. He wrote of investing in youth as the best way "to invest in the future." He said he had previously "never thought of the principal as the instructional leader," and now understood that concept. He wanted those who worked for him to "want to work for the kids and for what's in the best interest of the kids." He viewed himself as "an advocate for kids," and believed strongly that unless we make a positive investment in youth, we are at risk of losing them.

Becoming a good leader was important to Ross. He expressed the belief that leadership begins with self-understanding and that careful analysis of oneself, as well as the organization, is a necessary precursor to leadership effectiveness. He wrote that he wanted to be effective, effi-cient, and "consciously competent in my job," and he believed that paying attention to people, will cause them to "perform better." He also identified balance in his life and enjoyment of life as personal priorities.

Espoused Theory: As a Leader. Ross began his principalship in 1994, at Vineyard Middle School. This school, in rural central California, was a school with a long way to go. It was reputed to be in a community with the lowest per capita income in the state, a 97% Hispanic population, essentially no sense of community in the tiny town made up primarily of agricultural workers, a history of poor education, and reading scores virtually in the basement. Principal Ross Williams knew that the only way he could move his school was up. Ross had a vision for Vineyard, even before he left his prior job as a high school assistant principal to go there. When he took the reins as principal, he told himself that he wanted Vineyard to become a California Distinguished School within 5 years. He did not tell his staff at that time; he has not told them yet.

As a graduate student, Ross had written that he was concerned when people "make changes before [they] know what is wrong or where [they] want to go." As a principal, now, he feels he understands change and what is required to lead this school in new directions. He understands its organizational culture and how it must be carefully shaped. And, perhaps, most important, he believed then, and he believes now, that people affected by changes must be involved in those changes and must be "comfortable" with them if "cooperative efforts" are to evolve.

In the personal interview, Ross identified these guiding values in his life: "relationships," "treating others as I want to be treated," "providing a good education for kids," and "respect and responsibility."

He wants to be a catalyst for a model school and to spark the enthusiasm of the staff. He wishes to provide "a learning climate that will motivate students to seek knowledge and understanding and to become productive members of society." Ross knows that he needs to continue seeking balance in his life and that time for reflection is important.

Ross is living his dreams. Although it has not been easy, he is finding rewards in the process. Much of his first year was spent in supervising the rebuilding of several classrooms, which were destroyed, it was believed, by an arson fire. His background in teaching carpentry and construction was extremely helpful, but the demands on his time were considerable. His school also faced a state compliance review in his first year and an academic review in the second. Although leading these review processes was very demanding, he learned much about Vineyard and its teachers, programs, students, and community. The Vineyard community learned about him as well.

Developing a team of people is a slow process, but Ross believes progress is being made in teachers' willingness to try new ideas (technology, for example) and work together (jointly developing a core curriculum). He is quite conscious of where he is going and how he is trying to bring teachers along. Given the history of negativism at the school before his arrival, he says, "I have to be careful. I can't have a setback. I can't lose trust." He believes the "timing" has not yet been right for the joint development of a mission. Very soon, he will talk more to his teachers about outcomes for kids and what that means. He thinks this may be the year that they create a mission for Vineyard. It may even be the year he tells them about his own vision for the school, as he thinks they are ready to hear it now.

Ross is a man who uses symbols and symbolic behavior to his advantage. When this interviewer visited him in his office, he illustrated his use of symbols in leadership by displaying a basket full of 100 or more keys, which he keeps on his desk. This is what his predecessor left him—a school with a burned-out building and a huge pile of unmarked keys—and he is constantly reminded of how he found the school and where he intends to take it. He recounted a story about his opening talk to teachers in which he told an upbeat story in which apples represented teachers and their good work. He gave each teacher an apple to eat during the rest of the meeting. Whether they all understood his message is debatable; his purpose was to begin a journey with them in which they knew they were valued by him.

Ross values relationships and works hard to foster positive ones. He treats his teachers as he would want to be treated. He has instituted an end-of-year party at his home, a tradition that is growing in popularity and becoming a part of the culture. He works hard to "build trust among the staff and with each other" and "to emphasize working for the good of the kids."

Ross mentioned the loneliness of the principalship and the importance for him of meeting with other school leaders as he can find the time. The job may not be all that he expected, and he is climbing a considerable mountain, but as he described his work and his dreams for the school, he seemed confident about his approach to the position and the school.

Theory in Use: Teachers' Perceptions. Teachers at Vineyard Middle School, while representing some variety in opinion about their principal's leadership, seem to understand that he has plans for this school, and, for the most part, they are positive about their role in changes being made.

Faculty identified his values as "encouraging respect in kids" and "honoring teachers, students." One teacher was unsure about Ross's values; another said that he "tries to win us, tactfully."

While his teachers are uncertain about empowerment and what it might mean, some noted that they had "open discussions" with him, that he "facilitates" and does not "dictate," that they "feel more at ease," and "not threatened," and that "trust is building." Two teachers noted that about 20% of the staff is not part of the team and tend to be critical; one said there are "pockets of team spirit," and that teachers are always "there for each other." It was noted that the "atmosphere is improving" and "We are getting together socially; we like that."

The school's mission has not yet been developed by the current staff. Most, however, now understand Ross's desire to move Vineyard forward. "He may have Blue Ribbon School status in mind," said one, and others commented that his interest is in "improving student academic achievement," in "making kids better readers," and in creating an "exemplary school." One thought he had "big plans" and said that he had shared some of them with her. Two were not sure of his vision for the school.

In terms of the principal's influence on the organizational context, Ross was said by one to be "a breath of fresh air, a great influence." Another said, "He's on the right track; we're becoming." One said Ross had not been there long enough and he "needs to be more forceful." Still another said that people feel "valuable, useful." And it was noted that the principal "encourages and supports us," and "feels comfortable around people."

Case Perspective. Although Ross's values as a student may have been somewhat general, he knew what he wanted and believed in. Perhaps his experience as teacher, counselor, and assistant principal helped him develop a strong sense of his beliefs. Today, he seems to be living his values, and, for the most part, his teachers recognize and understand what is important to him. Table 3.3 points to the congruence between his earlier espoused theory and his theory in use as perceived by his teachers. His concern for excellence in the organizational setting has been a common theme in his leadership. Excellence is defined by Ross as academic achievement, and his concern for efficiency and exemplary performance based on institutional standards is reflective of the machine metaphor. However, there is a keen interest in human growth and improvement, which moves him toward a more organistic approach. Ross appears to be functioning at the Institutional Cycle of growth and phase two of values consciousness.

Ross's teachers know that he is vitally interested in the welfare and learning of students. They see him as "a teacher," one who understands young people and the difficulties of the community in which they all work. And this provides him with credibility. While one or two have some complaints about his "failure" to be more directive or to have been unduly influenced in his first year by "some people," teachers generally respect him as a leader. They seem to like him. They are willing to follow

Table 3.3. Analysis of Leadership Values Espoused and Reflected in Leadership Behavior: Ross

Motto	Term/Phrases Espoused	Behaviors Noted by Faculty	Organizational Metaphors	Growth Cycle and Values Consciousness Stage
"Education is the golden ticket. It is an investment in human capital. What better way to invest in our future than by investing in our youth."	My job is to prepare students for the future and for their place in a democracy To be effective, efficient, and consciously competent in my job To be a catalyst for a model school To promote technology and the core curriculum	He wants his school to shine, to do something special and have people know it He desires to improve student academic achievement Wants school to become exemplary Understands community	<u>Machine</u> Efficiency Productivity Excellence <u>Organism</u> Improvement Growth	Institutional Cycle: Adherence to authority symbolized in institutions Phase Two Values Consciousness: Desire to belong not only within family and social groups, but to organizations; schools seen as "families," with emphasis on collegiality

him. And some, in spite of its history, are even excited about the future of Vineyard.

No doubt his many years in education have served Ross well and prepared him for this role. His leadership classes and the chance to work collaboratively in a cohort, to reflect, to practice with feedback, and to discuss issues and practices in his fieldwork seem to have prepared him well for his role as a principal. His is a tough job. He reported that he kept his platform near him and used it as he planned his meetings with staff, particularly the opening of school meetings, so important to setting the tone for the year. If he can "fulfill the promise" to the children of California's Central Valley (the theme of the new Valley League of Schools, of which he is an Executive Board member), he will have made a difference in the lives of kids and teachers. A large percentage of children in the Central Valley of California live in extreme poverty and face issues of ill health, lack of basic necessities, exhausted parents, and a lack of understanding of the educational system or resources available to assist families. The kind of leadership Ross believes in and practices can serve the poor community of Vineyard well. The children, families, and teachers need someone who believes in their potential success. They seem to be willing to let him lead and even to be involved in that leadership. His eye is on the future. He will have affected that as well.

Bob Crawford

As a graduate student, Bob Crawford wrote, "If we work together as a team, no one can impede what we are trying to accomplish." Prior to becoming principal, in 1995, of Patterson High School, a school situated in a rural mining and agricultural community in southwestern Colorado, Bob was a high school teacher and coach for 13 years. His original motivation for entering the leadership development program at the University of Northern Colorado was to become a central office administrator; however, his involvement in the 3-year program convinced him that he could have more influence on students as a school principal than by continuing as a teacher and coach or becoming a school district administrator.

Espoused Theory: As a Student. His extensive background in coaching athletic teams, along with recent experience as part of a university cohort, had a profound influence on how Bob saw school organizations needing to function. Bob believed that people must work together to provide a quality education for students and that "teamwork is needed if teachers are to reach the next step in their development."

Bob espoused a belief that education should provide students with opportunities to develop into productive members of society. He viewed teachers as facilitators of this learning—as guides rather than sages—and believed that administrators should promote a climate of optimism rather than negativity in their support of teachers' efforts. Administrators should be controlled, organized, and industrious team members willing to take risks and model strong values.

Espoused Theory: As a Leader. Bob was beginning his second year as principal of Patterson, a high school of approximately 200 students with 20 full- and part-time teaching staff, only two of them over the age of 40. The school has one assistant principal, who also serves as the counselor and athletic director. The Patterson community comprises mainly working-class families, many of whom are employed by the local mining company or are involved in the agricultural business. Many students are motivated to complete high school so they will be eligible for jobs at the mine or with local businesses. Parents want their children to succeed in high school, but Bob feels they may not demand the level of performance (A and B work) that he and the school's teachers would expect.

Before Bob's arrival at Patterson, the school and the local community gradually had become separated. Many parents and community members did not feel directly connected with the school. The former principal rarely attended athletic events away from the school and avoided local business organizations, such as the Kiwanis, Rotary Club, and Chamber of Commerce.

After a year in the role of school principal, Bob seems to have as much passion, energy, and enthusiasm for being a school leader as when he finished his preparation program. In the interview, his statements captured much of his earlier enthusiasm and point out the high level of commitment he brings to his role.

Bob is clear about what he believes and values. To be sure, the daily interactions and events experienced by a high school principal can challenge a person's ability to live out those values. He acknowledges that living in a small community makes him more aware of the importance of keeping certain information confidential. His desire to be honest with others conflicts with the need to avoid revealing sensitive information that might be misinterpreted or misused by others. Furthermore, as a first-year principal, he is trying to be more visible and model certain behaviors; these actions reduce his popularity with some educators.

Although Bob is not one to take credit for what has transpired at Patterson, he does acknowledge a number of contributions he has made. For example, he believes that students and teachers have more pride in their work and in the school. Students are more cooperative and fewer disciplinary problems arise now that a consistent and effective discipline plan has been implemented. He believes that the community feels more a part of the school again and that teachers are growing professionally. He believes, too, that his efforts at team building are beginning to show results. Teachers are coming to Bob with ideas and suggestions for improving the school. He senses that his espoused belief that "teachers make the difference" seems to be having an impact on how staff see their individual and collective efforts to make Patterson a more productive learning environment for students and adults. He sees that his continuing challenge is to move teachers to the "next level" where they will be able to become a more effective team that bonds together. To achieve this goal, he believes he will need to continue to provide the vision or direction for the school and build trust so that meaningful relationships and bonds can develop.

Bob acknowledges his cohort experience and resulting opportunities for self-awareness as a decided influence in his development as a leader. His sense is that the three-summer experience allowed him to learn how to develop and reach a vision, built his self-confidence and sense of efficacy, and provided a sense of support and security needed for growth. Although Bob acknowledges the importance of this experience in his life and development as a school leader, his determination to ensure that Patterson becomes an effective learning environment for students and adults speaks highly of his ability to practice the values he clarified in his earlier platform and the skills he developed during the preparation program. Bob senses the faculty, staff, and students realize the direction he is headed in, but he knows that the school has a long way to go to reach the level of excellence he desires.

Theory in Use: Teachers' Perceptions. Staff members shared their impressions of Bob's views on the purpose of education as well as what he expects of teachers, administrators, and students. They sense Bob's view of education is that students should be actively involved in learning, accountable and responsible for their actions, and introduced to the realities of life so that they are prepared for the future, whether they choose to attend college or enter the workforce. They believe Bob is extremely interested in the future success of all students, regardless of background or previous history in the educational system.

To ensure these student outcomes are achieved, teachers must "coach and sponsor" students, providing them with numerous opportunities to become actively involved in the curriculum. They feel Bob has encouraged their efforts to develop a hands-on, experiential curriculum, citing his support of the technology curriculum and the integrated studies program.

In addition, faculty report that Bob views teachers not as merely presenting lessons to students, but as people who should be involved in school-level decision making, including the hiring of staff, scheduling classes, redesigning the curriculum, and participation in community activities and events.

One staff member suggests Bob is an "environmental engineer," constantly working to create a climate supportive of change and innovation. By getting input from staff and being sensitive to their needs, Bob is seen as creating such a climate. For instance, faculty noted the significance of his visiting all staff members (cooks, custodians, clerical and teaching staff) during the summer prior to his first year as principal. During these visits, he gathered their ideas about what the school needed to accomplish. In addition, his sensitivity to staff members' needs is illustrated by his willingness to alter a teacher's schedule so she could go home during the noon hour to nurse her new child. They note that Bob expects students always to give their best in academics, athletics, and citizenship. He wants students to know their strengths and take advantage of the opportunities afforded by the school and the community. They sense that his immediate and matter-of-fact style of dealing with disciplinary matters demonstrates to students that he not only cares about their actions, but that he also does not carry a grudge after the disciplinary incident is over.

Although a sense of team spirit existed before Bob became principal, he has helped staff members become even more involved in working together. By constantly praising staff for their accomplishments, Bob reveals his eagerness to see them grow and develop their talents. Not only has the staff continued to host potluck dinners and baby showers for staff members, but Bob also has involved them in making school-level decisions, such as asking for input on hiring new teachers and developing the master schedule, issues that teachers rarely had input into before.

His willingness to support the staff's ideas and involve them in decision making has enhanced the staff's sense of ownership and empowerment in the school's affairs. They feel one of Bob's greatest assets is his ability to listen to their ideas, assess their needs, and respond quickly. An important consequence of being so approachable is that Bob learns of problems before they become crises. Staff members are likely to tell Bob about sensitive situations so he can be alerted to potential problems rather than being blindsided by them. His ability to listen and his consistent approach have been especially important in resolving the disciplinary problems that existed when Bob arrived at Patterson. For example, one of his first actions was to produce a written discipline code, which he has implemented "fairly and evenhandedly," according to staff members.

Students and teachers know what the consequences are for infractions; Bob follows these policies and takes immediate action.

The staff see Bob moving the school in important directions in the future. An integral part of Bob's vision for the school is his desire to see Patterson High receive a Blue Ribbon School award within the next 2 years. This highly competitive national award recognizes schools that demonstrate excellence and quality for students and staff. He has told staff that in his mind they already are performing like a Blue Ribbon School, and he wants them to be recognized for their accomplishments. Such recognition not only would be important for staff morale, but also would demonstrate to the local community the worth of the school, a matter of continuing importance to the staff.

Staff members are quick to point out the values that underscore Bob's words and actions. They see him wanting what is best for teachers and students by valuing involvement, effort, creativity, and a diversity of instructional approaches. His core values are fairness and honesty in dealing with people. The contributions Bob has made to the school in his short tenure are revealed in the major themes presented above. In particular, staff members feel his most significant contributions include his consistent approach to dealing with people and problems, and his willingness to support people professionally and personally. For example, his follow-through with discipline has shown them there is "substance behind his words." In addition, Bob supports staff by listening to their curricular ideas, obtaining equipment and resources, and encouraging staff to take mental health days to ensure they maintain their vitality and enthusiasm for the job. Initially, some staff and students sensed Bob's exuberance as sometimes lacking sincerity; however, as he toned down his excitement and took positive steps toward the goals he spoke of, they became convinced that his actions were sincere and matched his words.

Case Perspective. Overall, there is considerable consistency among many of the ideals Bob expressed in the educational platform he produced in his leadership preparation program, his stated goals and aspirations for Patterson, and the impression of staff members as to what he stands for and is trying to accomplish. Table 3.4 displays this congruence and the overarching emphasis on teamwork. Bob's emphasis on planned and structured procedures suggest the machine metaphor; however, this tendency is balanced with his more humanistic ideals of growth and connectedness. He exhibits the best characteristics of the Institutional Cycle and phase two of values consciousness.

Staff members see Bob's views about the purpose of education the same way he does. While Bob emphasizes "real-world" learning experi-

Table 3.4. Analysis of Leadership Values Espoused and Reflected in Leadership Behavior: Bob

Motto	Terms/Phrases Espoused	Behaviors Noted by Faculty	Organizational Metaphors	Growth Cycle and Values Consciousness Stage
"If we work together as a team, no one can impede what we are trying to accomplish."	Teamwork, working together, facilitating cooperation Productivity Consistency Structure Organizational control	Involves staff in decisions Supports teachers Ensures that students are actively involved, accountable, and responsible Demonstrates to the community the worth of the school Emphasizes productivity through people	Machine Efficiency Productivity Organization Structure Organism Connectedness Growth Communication	Institutional Cycle: Adherence to authority symbolized in institutions Phase Two Values Consciousness: Desire to belong not only within family and social groups, but to organizations; schools seen as "families," with emphasis on collegiality and a sense of belonging

ences, his staff senses that Bob values involvement, accountability, and responsibility so that the future workplace needs of students will be met.

Bob stresses the facilitative role teachers play. Teachers understand this emphasis and recognize that their principal sees them as being responsible for a variety of tasks beyond classroom instruction. Both Bob and his staff report that his role as a school administrator is a supportive one. Staff members believe Bob is attempting to create a climate for change (e.g., the "environmental engineer" analogy) and is sensitive to their professional and personal needs. Bob feels that teachers and other staff members are taking more pride in their efforts as a result of his encouragement. Although staff members do not mention self-pride when speaking of his supportive attitude, they indicate "feeling at ease" and being less tense because of his support for their individual and collective efforts. Both Bob and the staff describe the school as operating as an interrelated system, which is a more organic or holistic approach to viewing organizations. Bob uses the concept of teamwork to describe this interdependency; staff members use other images (e.g., the "MASH unit" analogy).

Comparing the espoused ideals in Bob's leadership platform with his desired goals for Patterson High, and then analyzing the impressions of staff members concerning Bob's actions, reveals a fairly consistent pattern. When interviewed, Bob was more precise about what he was attempting to accomplish at Patterson than he had been as a student. Undoubtedly, this was because he was describing an actual school setting, rather than a more general philosophy as articulated in his platform. Regardless of the level of specificity, however, there is still consistency in his espoused views. These views are further validated in his leadership behavior.

Comparisons Across Subjects

Various themes emerged from the portraitures. The themes, or values, include valuing concrete, real-world experiences; recognizing one's social responsibility and promoting that value through education; nurturing others in their struggles to become; promoting connectedness or shared learning; valuing growth and continual personal development; and fostering renewal, change, and creativity through one's own initiative.

As a means of reflecting on the values that each leader espoused most frequently, key terms and phrases stressed by each of the leaders and their staff have been identified. Tables 3.1–3.4 presented an analysis of the leaders, including their central message, or motto; the key phrases that they espoused; and phrases expressed by members of their staff in describing their behavior. In addition, the organizational metaphor that they seemed to espouse along with the cycle of growth and phase of values consciousness most indicative of their behavior were presented. In all cases, these leaders showed consistency between their espoused theories and their theories in use. Likewise, each leader was shown to be progressing positively toward higher levels of values growth and consciousness.

OVERALL PERSPECTIVES

The portraitures suggest that the espoused values of these leaders during the time of their leadership preparation have remained consistent with the values they currently espouse and with the values that are exhibited in their leadership behavior. Although each leader espouses a somewhat different view of the leadership role and the underlying values supporting that view, each has carved out a place of leadership that appears to be effective and one that is uniquely his or her own. This lends support to the concept of leadership artistry conveyed by Kouzes and Posner (1987) and suggests that there is worth in clarifying one's values through such activities as platform development. If leadership is an extension of what the individual values and if it is effectively orchestrated as that individual becomes more self-aware and accepting, then leadership development programs need to cultivate opportunities for deep personal and interpersonal reflection to occur.

Some Ideas to Consider

If the values articulated and developed during leadership preparation do remain a central part of a leader's theory in use, it is important that opportunities exist within preparation programs for a more deliberate and thoughtful approach to values clarification. The platform, developed in a cohort or community setting where feedback and assistance are provided by faculty and student colleagues, appears to be an important tool to assist in this process. In addition, the prospects for connecting the platform to other meaningful learning experiences, many of which are described in Chapter 5, are numerous.

Attention might be given to the following points when considering the use of educational platforms:

1. Platforms should be constructed in the context of self-awareness activities such as personality/leadership assessments and develop-

ment of individualized educational plans (Norris, Basom, Yerkes, & Barnett, 1996).

2. Platforms should be directly integrated with the academic content related to leadership, organizational theory, curriculum and instruction, and cultural awareness (Norris, Herrmond, & Meisgeier, 1996).

3. Platform elements may include the aims of education, major achievements of students in the current year, the social significance of students' learning, the image of the learner, the image of the curriculum, the image of the teacher, the preferred pedagogy, and the preferred school climate. Supervisors may choose to add the purpose or goals of supervision and the preferred process of supervision (Sergiovanni & Starratt, 1993).

4. Platforms should serve as a reflection tool for validating the solutions to problem-solving activities, examining leadership projects, and understanding positions taken on educational issues (Norris, Basom, Yerkes, & Barnett, 1996).

5. Platforms should be revisited in discussion and reflection sessions within cohort settings. Free exchange of ideas should take place in a climate of support and trust (Norris, Basom, Yerkes, & Barnett, 1996).

6. Platforms should be viewed as dynamic entities subject to modification and elaboration as personal growth occurs. They should be reviewed periodically as the student moves through the preparation program (Barnett, 1991).

7. Platforms should be used as a basis for developing educational visions and preparing students for future leadership positions (Barnett, 1991).

If, as some believe, school improvement models are deficit models, then why not consider that leaders can indeed effect change in schools once they can understand themselves and others? If university faculty, through particular activities and behaviors, can influence students' self-understanding and personal, as well as professional, development, could that not have an impact on graduates' leadership of schools? If, as Sergiovanni and Starratt (1993) suggest, a reflective document such as an educational platform tends to shape the educator's everyday practice, cannot such reflective activities actually inform the work of education professionals? If, as Hall and his colleagues (1991) propose, people cannot move to higher levels until they have the means to do so, and if, as Covey (1989) writes, one cannot lead at any higher level than that at which he or she is functioning, then cannot perhaps the development of values consciousness and reflection in a community environment in graduate education programs contribute to the improvement of schools?

IN SUMMARY

We are convinced that leadership development programs must address the concepts of values clarification and the building of communities. As our society embraces the notions of transformational leadership, collaborative work, and communities of learners, principled leaders will be crucially needed to orchestrate cooperation and connectedness among individuals. As fewer educators are choosing to enter the ranks of school administration, those who do are expected to be far more than managers or transactional leaders. Their understanding and ability to practice the necessary skills based on their beliefs, values, practices, and preparation will determine their credibility. The credibility of today's and tomorrow's transformational leaders, in turn, will determine their influence on America's schools.

4

Transformational Leadership: Conceptualized and Developed

> Caring . . . is an orientation of deep concern
> that carries us out of ourselves, and into the
> lives, despairs, struggles, and hopes of others.
> —Nel Noddings

LEADERSHIP IS a moral act that considers the welfare of those under one's care and fosters improved conditions for their human existence. A "servant leader" (Greenleaf, 1977) orientation lies at the heart of transformational leadership; its foundation rests firmly on the notion of community. This chapter acknowledges the moral imperatives of leadership (Goodlad, 1984; Norris & Barnett, 1994) and challenges future educational leaders, and those who orchestrate their development, to serve as catalysts for establishing learning communities designed to promote a sense of mutual care and responsibility.

In this chapter, we contrast this transformational leadership perspective with more authoritative leadership views perpetuated by traditional practices and outdated educational administration philosophies. We explore this new leadership paradigm—one that embraces community—and consider appropriate avenues that preparation programs can employ to instill its principles in the hearts and minds of future leaders. We begin our discussion by exploring the concepts of moral leadership and the ethic of care, foundations for this emerging paradigm.

MORAL LEADERSHIP THROUGH CARE

Care is a practice as well as a disposition that causes individuals to act on the basis of the needs and concerns of others (Gilligan, 1982). It is central to the notion of community for it "reflects a cumulative knowledge of human relationships and evolves around a central insight, that self and others are interdependent" (Gilligan, 1982, p. 74). Caring leaders recognize that responsibility to others extends beyond merely establishing good interpersonal relationships with students, staff, and parents. Leaders who live and learn within community become aware that moral and social responsibilities are deeply rooted in the concept of leadership. They develop a deep desire to make a difference in the lives of others, and this desire extends beyond their immediate circle of influence to encompass a broader social arena (Foster, 1986). Transformational leaders recognize that they are, indeed, responsible for influencing more humane conditions, not only within their immediate school settings but also throughout the broader educational environment and culture.

A review of Hall's (1976) model of values consciousness, presented in Chapter 2, helps to clarify this expanded concept of leadership. Table 4.1 relates the values consciousness model (Hall, 1976) to the Ethic of Care Perspectives theorized by Gilligan (1982).

Each perspective of care—care of self, care of others, and care of self and others—has a transition, or awareness, stage that moves the individual to the next perspective (Gilligan, 1982). In the first perspective, care of self, the individual is aware only of his or her own needs, particularly the needs for safety and security. During this time, as in the first stage of Hall's model, the individual has a desire to preserve self and to be secure. Since self is the center of the person's world, the needs of others pale in comparison to the concerns that the individual has for his or her own needs. As the individual gains more self-understanding and increases his or her understanding of others, interpersonal relations improve—the individual acquires the means for accomplishing the next level of values

Table 4.1. Gilligan's Ethic of Care Perspectives Compared with Hall's Cycles and Phases of Consciousness

Ethic of Care	*Values Cycle*	*Phase of Consciousness*
Self	Primal	Phase One
	Familial	
	Institutional	Phase Two
Others	Interpersonal	Phase Three
Self and others	Communal/collaborative	
	Mystical	Phase Four

awareness and goal attainment (Hall, 1976) and a new perspective of care emerges (Gilligan, 1982). The focus on self begins to shift to a focus on others. Thus, in the first transition from care of self to care of others, the person, who has focused primarily on self, begins to question that behavior and to feel more responsibility toward others.

That individual who has learned to care from a perspective of others moves beyond a care for self and displays a genuine interest in the welfare and development of others. While this shift in care focus seems admirable and altruistic, it does have its disadvantages to an individual's overall development as a person. Some individuals, operating from this perspective, become almost consumed with the interests and demands of others. Many care givers, or persons in service occupations such as nursing, counseling, and teaching, find that they are so involved with their clients' needs that they have little time left for self (Maslach, 1982). Religious teachings sometimes have tended to foster this notion of selflessness as a noble enterprise. The individual long operating from a care of others perspective finally reaches a point where some balance must be found and attention given to his or her own needs.

In transition two, the person who previously focused exclusively on others begins to feel some discomfort at the imbalance that this perspective has created and moves to the next perspective, care of self and others. It is important to note that the individual does not at this point abandon a care of others perspective but instead adds to it a concern for the welfare of self. This stage is a perspective of universal care that is in line with Hall's highest phases of values consciousness, the Communal/Collaborative and Mystical cycles.

We believe that the means for developing values consciousness goals, or level of care perspectives, are enhanced through community. In other words, individuals learn to care as they are given opportunities to become more aware of others and to develop the skills that enable better interaction and enhanced knowledge of others. Communities contribute back to individuals by assisting them in recognizing and appreciating their own needs for care. A look back at the comments of our students in Chapter 1 supports these transitions and connects them to the learning community model. Table 4.2 compares the models of Hall and Gilligan with the learning community model discussed in Chapter 1.

An ethic of care, then, is an ethic that supports community in its truest sense—individuals and groups working for their mutual benefit. Community, in turn, provides individuals with the means, or skills, necessary to become aware at higher levels of values consciousness and more mature perspectives of care. But what is care, and what moral implications does it have for leadership?

Table 4.2. Individual Development Within Learning Community Compared with Gilligan's Ethic of Care Perspectives and Hall's Cycles and Phases of Consciousness

Individual Development	*Ethic of Care*	*Values Cycle*	*Phase of Consciousness*
Security	Self	Primal	Phase One
Support		Familial	
		Institutional	Phase Two
Friendship	Others	Interpersonal	Phase Three
Knowledge	Self and others	Communal/ collaborative	
Personal Dream		Mystical	Phase Four

ETHIC OF CARE

It is common within the educational arena to toss the word *care* about as though being a "caring person" is a given for everyone in the educational field. The notions of "loving children," being driven by "higher purposes," or being "altruistic" may, or may not, be absolutes connected to the profession of teaching or school administration. "It is possible that what we might describe as 'caring work' can be done without a caring disposition" (Beck, 1994, p. 105). It is possible that not all teachers or administrators do care. It is possible, also, that educators may not care at the same level of awareness or concern. What, then, is care and how might we recognize the depth of care possessed?

The concept of care is best understood by considering its phases of development. Care is demonstrated in four phases: (1) caring about, (2) taking care of, (3) care giving, and (4) care receiving (Gilligan, 1982). These phases represent increased levels of awareness and suggest the depth to which one values the notion. The evolution of the value of care is in line with the values acquisition theory discussed in Chapter 2. Individuals, as they develop the care value, move from receiving, to responding, to valuing, and finally to characterizing that value (Krathwohl, 1964). We examine each level and discuss the implications of each for leadership.

Caring about is the first level of care and it involves recognizing that care is really necessary. It is a values receiving stage (Krathwohl, 1964) in which the leader becomes aware of another's need and gives it some initial attention. Caring about is actually empathizing, or experiencing with another what it is like to be in their position. Educational leaders at this stage of care might ask themselves questions such as: What is it truly like to be a member of this ethic group or this gender, to live in this home, to have these parents, to teach in this classroom? Recently, a student in one of our learning communities expressed this level of care as he considered situations within his school. He wrote the following comment in his reflective journal:

> My questions for this reflection are as follows: How does it feel for a special needs student to come to school knowing that no one cares? How does it feel to come to school hungry or alone? How does it feel to come to school for safety and support because there is none at home? I do not know the answers to any of these questions and I am thankful that my sons will never have to know them either. I do know I want to answer the questions as an administrator, or at least find a solution that decreases the number of children asking themselves so many questions. I want to challenge my staff to walk a few steps in the tiny shoes of our students.

Taking care of is the next level of care. Leaders at this level actually assume some of the responsibility for those in need by becoming proactive and committed to seeing that care is provided. Care extends beyond merely "caring about" to taking action to ensure that care is provided. Something is actually done to intervene—to right the wrongs, to correct the injustice, to see that a service is provided. The leader responds (Krathwohl, 1964).

Care giving, the third level of care, involves directly meeting the needs for care, doing the actual work, and coming into contact with the actual person for whom one cares. Leaders at this stage take the time to care. This means that leaders take an active part in the person's care by spending the time it takes with teachers, with students, and with parents who have a need. Care giving has become a personal value (Krathwohl, 1964).

Care receiving is the final phase of care, and it involves recognizing that the object of care will respond to the care received. Leaders appreciate the vulnerability of those who receive care and do not take advantage of those who depend on them. At this stage of caring, leaders have progressed to levels of organizing and characterizing their values (Krathwohl, 1964). Caring in its fullest sense has become a way of life.

True care, then, becomes the basis of what Greenleaf (1977) has termed "servant leadership." Servant leadership carries with it a commitment to be of service to those in one's care and grows out of the leader's personal regard and care for others.

SERVANT LEADERSHIP

Greenleaf (1977) places the concept of the servant leader at the highest levels of care: care giving and care receiving. He describes the servant leader as one who "does their [care receivers'] menial chores, but who also sustains them with his spirit and his song" (p. 7). The servant leader is not only actively involved in the group's care, but also lifts group members' spirits and "encourages the heart" (Kouzes & Posner, 1987). Such leaders bring hope and encouragement to others as they work together in community. As we have observed our students in learning communities over the past few years, we have been especially impressed with their ability to sustain one another—to challenge the heart and encourage the spirit. The atmosphere of a learning community truly allows future leaders to experience the joy and excitement of working together in collegial spirit to accomplish tasks. Students learn that true leaders are an integral part of the group—not separated from it. There is mutual concern and a spirit of genuine care. Certainly in the field of education, the most human of all enterprises, there should be community settings that exude care. Teachers and administrators should genuinely care about one another and about the students and parents that they serve. Care is a necessary component of any organization that provides service to others. That feeling is captured well in the following statement:

> Any human service where the one who is served should be loved in the process requires community, a face-to-face group in which the liability of each for the other and all for one is unlimited, or as close to it as it is possible to get. . . . Living in community as one's basic involvement will generate an exportable surplus of love which the individual may carry into his many involvements with institutions which are usually not communities. (Greenleaf, 1977, p. 38)

But just responding with a caring attitude is not enough; leaders must be care givers.

The servant leader represents the moral leader, a care giver who is seen as a servant first. The concepts of "leader first" and "servant first" are totally opposite in meaning. "The servant-leader is servant first. It begins with the natural feeling that one wants to serve, to serve first" (Greenleaf, 1977, p. 13). Sergiovanni (1992) speaks of this same leadership quality in his discussion of "followership first, then leadership" (p. 67) and suggests that when followership is combined with leadership, the whole nature of the enterprise changes. There is no longer a bureaucratic hierarchy with the leader at the top; instead, the organization is based on followership and is guided by ideas, values, and commitments. The organization is transformed from its more traditional base of bureaucratic and technical-rational authority, described later in this chapter, to authority based on professional and moral principles. This authority base comes from the leader's "demonstrated devotion and success as a follower" (Sergiovanni, 1992, p. 67)—a perspective that allows many leaders to emerge and work together to influence the direction of the enterprise. Leaders become both followers as well as leaders; their roles are constantly changing. This notion is beautifully expressed in the following passage:

> Leadership, in the final analysis, is the ability of humans to relate deeply to each other in the search for a more perfect union. Leadership is a consensual task, a sharing of ideas and a sharing of responsibilities, where a leader is a leader for the moment only, where the followership exerted must be validated by the consent of the followers, and where leadership lies in the struggles of the community to find meaning for itself. (Foster, 1986, p. 61)

Certainly in true learning communities, individuals experience this shifting of leadership influence. They come to understand the gifts that people bring to the table, the beauty in diversity, the strength in shared meaning and purpose.

The servant leader is easily recognized for he or she takes great care to "make sure that other people's highest priority needs are being served. . . . The best test, and difficult to administer, is: Do those served grow as persons? Do they, while being served, become healthier, wiser, freer, more autonomous, more likely themselves to become servants?" (Greenleaf, 1977, p. 14). Servant leaders, then, are dedicated to the growth and development of others; they have the capacity to bring about personal and institutional change. Through exposure to servant leadership, others are inspired to grow and to become far more than they presently are. Leaders, too, grow in the process. Servant leadership promotes, indeed, a transformation in the lives of people and organizations—a transformation defined as: "one or more persons engaged with others in such a way that leaders and followers raise one another to higher levels of motivation and morality" (Burns, 1978, p. 20).

But until recently, a transformational leadership perspective has not been emphasized either in practice or in educational administration preparation programs. Past practices and programs may have, in fact, perpetuated a view of leadership quite contrary to the notions of care and servant leadership. To help us better understand how to design future preparation programs that address this emerging paradigm, it is important to look backward and to examine what has transpired that may be contrary to this view and what should occur if we are to support it.

FRAMING LEADERSHIP PERSPECTIVES

We will examine three leadership perspectives—transactional, transactional-transformational, and transformational—and relate each to the organizational metaphor (Morgan, 1986) suggested by its characteristics. Each leadership perspective and its accompanying metaphor will then be compared with Hall's (1976) values consciousness phases and leadership modes as shown in Table 4.3. As we discuss each leadership perspective, attention also will be directed toward the curriculum and instructional approaches that support its concepts.

Burns (1978) identified two styles of leadership quite contrary in nature, a transactional style and a transformational style. Transactional leadership he defined as a style negotiated through a rational contract between leader and subordinate. In return for specified privileges and rewards, the subordinate complies with certain rules, regulations, and procedures necessary to accomplish a particular organizational directive. Transformational leadership, on the other hand, engages followers through a deeper commitment, or covenant, guided by a purpose that is felt to mutually benefit the individual and the organization. These dichotomous views of leadership serve as the building blocks for the three leadership perspectives we will discuss.

Table 4.3. Hall's Phases and Cycles of Values Consciousness Compared with Leadership Modes

Values Phase	Cycle of Growth	Leadership Mode
Survival, security	Primal	Autocratic
Self-worth	Familial	Benevolent/authority
Self-competence	Institutional	Bureaucratic
Independence	Interpersonal	Enabling
New order	Communal/collaborative	Charismatic
Interdependence	Mystical	Servant
Rights/world order	Prophetic	Interdependent

As we explore these three differing perspectives, it is important also to consider the definition of "power" and its interpretation in each of these perspectives. Robert Dahl has defined power as "an ability to get another person to do something that he or she would not otherwise have done" (Morgan, 1986, p. 158). There are various sources of power that influence this behavior—some are externally imposed and others depend on the individual's inner desire to move in a particular direction. In either case, control serves as the leverage for compliance. In each of the three leadership perspectives that we will explore, there is a source of power that enables this control. In some instances, control is external and depends on the leader's ability to manipulate external rewards; in others, it is intrinsic and depends on the leader's ability to influence others to desire to comply or to be influenced based on their own free will. In the first instance, the leader reacts in a passive, impersonal way by managing the people and tasks to produce a particular outcome determined by organizational mandate or policy. In the last instance, leading is the modus operandi (Zaleznik, 1977). In that role, the leader influences organizational direction in a proactive, personal way enabling both individual and organizational enhancement. In the section that follows, we consider the various leadership perspectives and discuss the manner in which power and control are enacted in each.

LEADERSHIP PERSPECTIVES, PAST AND PRESENT

Transactional Leadership

In this leadership perspective, the organization, with the leader at the apex, operates from a single-loop learning perspective (Argyris, 1957). A norm is established for the organization, generally based on established practices or policy. The leader's role, then, is to monitor compliance with that norm and to take corrective action when necessary to realign conditions with the previously determined norm. The subordinate understands the task and takes responsibility for compliance out of a sense of duty; the leader reciprocates with external rewards. Tasks and responsibilities are tightly defined and determined by top-down directives. There is little emotional commitment involved in this exchange, and subordinates generally work from a routine, disconnected perspective (Sergiovanni, 1990). Certainly, in this example of classical management theory the machine metaphor is very much in evidence. As shown in Table 4.3, the leader operates from a survival phase of values consciousness, with the means for this values phase centering on keeping self and the organization safe, secure, and uncomplicated. This survival phase of values consciousness is expressed in behavior indicative of the Authoritative or Benevolent Leader.

Chris Argyris (1957) talked of the immaturity that such an approach reinforces. Certainly it does little to foster independence or personal growth. Instead, it keeps subordinates in an immature state and fails to provide them the means for becoming conscious of higher values levels or goals. Not only do leaders operate out of a sense of insecurity with increased dependence on structure, policy, and organizational directives, but their followers do as well. In fact, in many instances, followers become more and more dependent on those in authority and look to them to provide the security that they do not feel intrinsically (Argyris, 1957).

Leadership preparation programs have been criticized for their own tendency to replicate this model in educational administration classrooms designed to prepare future school leaders (Murphy, 1990). Programs have been criticized for being professor-centered, based on standardized curriculum—or a "one best approach" to administrative preparation—and dependence on a behavioral science model that relates little to the technical or conceptual skills needed for administration of education (Cooper & Boyd, 1987; Griffiths, Stout, & Forsyth, 1988; Murphy, 1990). In a professor-centered instructional model, students are given little opportunity to move beyond a dependent state since the emphasis is focused heavily on the accumulation of knowledge that is passed down rather than elicited from the learner.

Transactional-Transformational Perspective

The second perspective, sometimes called a value-added approach (Bass, 1985; Sergiovanni, 1990), is both transactional *and* transformational. The theory behind this approach is that building onto a base of transactional leadership enables subordinates to build a foundation of readiness conducive to greater organizational participation. A transformational style of leadership is added at the point when the organization and its members have gained a foundation of stability and skill. This value-added component suggests that leaders shift from a more directive, or authoritarian, style to one that enables. Leaders in this phase of leadership foster a sense of purpose that inspires and motivates subordinates to "buy into" the organizational purpose and become committed to the goals of the organization.

The leader is still at the apex of the organization; however, subordinates are allowed to participate within the structure that has been set. This leadership view reflects Hall's Institutional values consciousness cycle of growth and the Bureaucratic leadership mode. It is important to note that leader and followers *both* have been elevated at this point to higher levels of values consciousness than they were at the transactional level. However, an investigation of Table 4.3 points out that there is still room for greater awareness and personal and organizational growth to occur.

The transactional-transformational leadership perspective has become quite popular in administrative preparation programs since the emphasis has been placed on the principal as instructional leader. The accountability movement has further strengthened this view. Table 4.3 reveals that this is an Institutional values consciousness cycle of growth, mediated by some attention being given to Independence and Interpersonal relationships. The task of leadership is still seen as being contained within a structure that depends on transactional leadership as its base. Leadership is still viewed as the domain of one individual primarily, and that individual operates from a structure outlined by the organization. Some have criticized this perspective, pointing out that it appears that transformational aspects are added on as a way of manipulating followers to "get the job done" and be happy and feel that they are contributing to the organizational purpose in the meantime. It is still basically a single-loop process, for rarely do subordinates, or even leaders, deviate from or question the norms that have been established.

Transformational Leadership

The final perspective of leadership to be considered is transformational leadership. This framework suggests that leadership and management are possibly two separate conditions that may or may not be the domain of one individual. Management is, of course, acknowledged and considered necessary to any organization and may or may not be the basic responsibility of the designated leader. Leadership, in contrast, can occur at any point in time and may be exerted by various stakeholders. Leadership is a shifting of influence that allows many followers to emerge as leaders at particular points in time. While leadership may be present with the designated leader, it is the domain of others as well. Leadership roles can shift so that the designated leader is both leader and follower, while the follower is both follower and leader. Individuals are empowered and in turn raise one another to higher levels of values consciousness (Foster, 1986; Norris, 1999; Sergiovanni, 1992).

ETHICAL RESPONSIBILITIES OF TRANSFORMATIONAL LEADERSHIP

Foster (1986) suggests that transformational leaders operate from four important characteristics: They are educational, critical, ethical, and transformational. In the educational role, they assist the organization in acquiring knowledge. Much of this knowledge acquisition has to do with discoveries about their own organization and its place in the wider environment of education and society. They challenge followers to consider questions about the school's history, the guiding values that have shaped its culture, the school's purpose, and how power is distributed throughout the organization (Foster, 1986). In this sense, leaders encourage team learning (Senge, 1990) and foster the dialogue that helps individuals make new connections and make better sense of the more global needs of the organization. These leaders are also concerned that followers have access to information from many sources and are provided opportunities for meaningful dialogue that will enhance their total knowledge and build new understandings. This in turn fosters a systems view (Senge, 1990), making individuals more aware of how situations or decisions in one part of the organization affect all others.

Second, transformational leaders are critical (Foster, 1986). They help organizational members take a closer look at current conditions within their schools and question the appropriateness of those situations for all students. In this regard, they help organizational members challenge the mental models (Senge, 1990) that may have repressed their very progress. They encourage problem finding—not just problem solving. They help organizations move beyond the status quo by encouraging a double-loop learning process (Argyris, 1957) that questions operating norms when they do not seem to be working, and readjusting organizational direction when it seems warranted. Such a model is proactive and dynamic, allowing the organization to grow and meet the expanding needs of its community. These leaders encourage individuals to care at deeper levels of human concern and to take action to correct conditions that appear to be unjust or inappropriate for others. These leaders help to build a sense of self-renewal that encompasses both individuals as well as the organization (Norris, 1999).

Third, these leaders are ethical (Foster, 1986). They encourage individuals to be reflective, to think about what they truly value, and to look for patterns of consistency between espoused values and demonstrated behavior. They encourage democratic values and moral relationships through an emphasis that includes both the ethic of justice and the ethic of care. These leaders strive to influence others to higher levels of values consciousness by providing them with the means for that attainment. At the same time, they remain open to their own values enhancement and to the development of means to encourage their awareness. These leaders and their followers are lifelong learners who encourage personal mastery (Senge, 1990) by causing community members to reflect upon their underlying values and beliefs and to come to understand what they truly do believe is right and appropriate.

Fourth, they are transformational. Their leadership is aimed toward social change through an elevation of human consciousness. They are aware that it is not enough to make people aware, but that they must provide others with the means that will encourage higher levels of values consciousness. These leaders seek to build a community of individuals who believe they can make a difference in the lives of those they touch. They help to promote a sense of shared vision (Senge, 1990) that not only raises awareness of what should be desired, but also establishes the means for accomplishing that vision. Transformational leadership, therefore, fosters all the dimensions of building a learning community (Senge, 1990). Transformational leaders not only serve but enable others to be servant leaders as well.

THE NEED FOR TRANSFORMATIONAL LEADERS

Indeed, we echo Goodlad's (1984) words that there are moral imperatives for leadership. As knowledge continues to expand and the gap between the advantaged and the disadvantaged increases, leaders will need to provide greater access to knowledge and opportunities to share knowledge throughout the organization. They will need to understand the importance of shared knowledge, of dialogue, and of drawing forth new knowledge as well as storing what is already known.

As cultural diversity expands, leaders will be called upon to question and correct unjust practices and to foster deeper connections between various groups. They will need to understand the importance of challenging mental models, of questioning current practice, and of fostering a deeper awareness of others and their needs.

As disengagement continues to be prevalent, leaders will need to build networks of care and concern, of mutual support and collegiality, and of continual learning that will challenge individuals and organizations to fulfill their maximum potential. They will need to understand deeply the concept of personal mastery and endeavor to promote the empowerment of self and others.

As demands for greater accountability increase, leaders will need to build frameworks for questioning the moral implications of existing practices and for conceptualizing visions of new directions. They will need to understand the importance of shared vision and ways to promote collaboration in the shaping of dreams for the future. The need for renewal will become increasingly important. Indeed, the need for transformational leaders will become all the more important as will the need for building the learning communities that foster their development. Greenleaf (1977) provides us with an optimistic look at the future possibilities of such transformation through community.

> The opportunities are tremendous for rediscovering vital lost knowledge about how to live in community. . . . All that is needed to rebuild community as a viable life form for a large number of people is for enough servant-leaders to show the way, not by mass movements, but by each servant-leader demonstrating his own unlimited liability for a quite specific community-related group. (p. 39)

Care seems to be a basic ingredient for transforming today's schools, and it seems to be cultivated and sustained through community. We believe that this is what happened in the cohorts that we studied—and what can happen in schools led by leaders who have themselves been part of a learning community. A student at the University of Houston recently posed the following question in her dissertation: Can principals learn to care? (Ballering, 1997). In response, we would add: Where will future leaders learn to care? We believe that administrator preparation programs have a tremendous responsibility to provide learning settings that promote a sense of care. It is important to note here that first professors must care!

A CHALLENGE TO THOSE WHO PREPARE LEADERS

Can we as professors afford our students with the same opportunities for growth and empowerment that we are asking them to provide to those they will one day lead? It is not enough to schedule a group and term it a "cohort" or "learning community." It is not enough to merely lecture within its structure. We as professors must design that learning experience as a true learning community. The key to that design actually lies within the concept of empowerment itself. In Chapter 2, we discussed the notion of empowerment. The three theories that support the concept of empowerment—needs, values, and thinking (Wasserman, 1991)—provide us with the dimensions needed for building meaningful learning communities. Each theory supporting empowerment serves as a guideline for the design of true learning communities, for each theory suggests what should be considered.

First, the learning experience should be designed on the basis of what truly meets the needs of our students. And what are those needs? Adult learning theory gives us a clear picture of the needs that adults have in a learning experience:

- Adults' self-concept requires that they be perceived as self-directing; therefore, they need increasing opportunities to direct their own learning.
- Adults' orientation to learning tends to be problem-centered rather than subject-centered.
- Adults have developed a rich reservoir of experiences that lead them to prefer less teacher transmittal of knowledge and more experiential learning opportunities.
- Adults' readiness to learn depends far more on the demands of their professional roles than on academic pressure (Knowles, 1980).

Aside from students' personal needs for quality learning, there are needs that the total community has in order to facilitate its fullest development. These include: opportunities to interact with one another, freedom to explore ideas, and autonomy to set goals and purposes for community learning. The curriculum should be shaped in ways that encourage students to search for meaning, to express varying views, to learn from each other through meaningful dialogue, to question practice, and to become problem finders—not just problem solvers.

Second, we should consider the values base on which we shape our learning communities. We need to encourage an ethic of care, an emphasis on inquiry and the right to question current practice, a search for meaning and purpose, and an emphasis on vision and renewal. And then there is process: How do we arrange the learning experience so that it enables the discovery and clarification of personal values and beliefs? How do we foster higher levels of espoused theory and theory in action? How do we develop credible leaders?

We must find ways, by recalling what has been learned about values, to ensure that these values are recognized. We must remember that values develop according to a hierarchy, that students must develop the means to fulfill values goals on the next level, that means develop before consciousness, that values shape the nature of groups, and that groups shape the nature of values.

Finally, we must consider the concept of thinking. What is our own philosophy of knowledge acquisition? Do we believe that knowledge exists in its final form and that we are mere dispensers of content, or do we believe instead that true knowledge grows out of dialogue and consideration of many ideas and viewpoints? Do we believe that knowledge is continually constructed through narratives and shared experiences and through exploration and new discoveries? Do we believe that learning is as much affective as it is cognitive? What do we truly believe is the purpose of education? What do we wish our product to be?

These are some of the questions that we must consider as we endeavor to provide our students with the means for their own empowerment as leaders. These are central questions that must be answered as we seek to design learning communities that will foster a new leadership paradigm. These are issues that will, in fact, be dealt with in the next chapter as we discuss the curriculum within the learning community.

5

Shaping the Curriculum to Foster Leadership Development Within Learning Communities

TODAY'S SCHOOLS have embraced the concept of community challenging leaders to serve as catalysts for individual and organizational transformations. If leadership is, indeed, the catalyst for creating organizational communities (Barnard, 1968a), how can future leaders, through their own educational preparation, be inspired to become catalysts for future institution building? This question forms the basis for this chapter.

In the following discussion we concentrate on the nature of the curriculum within learning communities. Curriculum is seen as having a dual purpose: (1) to explore the content, or knowledge base, that lends contextual understanding to the development of transformational leadership, and (2) to inform the process of developing a learning community through the acquisition and application of learning within community settings.

Universities must respond to the shifting leadership paradigm by redesigning preparation programs as leadership laboratories where curriculum is both content- and process-driven. It is feasible that the effective use of learning communities could provide the content, or knowledge base, necessary for this process, as well as reinforcement for the dispositions and performance skills necessary for that development (see the introduction for a description of the administrator preparation elements stressed in this book). Educational administration preparation programs will need to plan more deliberately and systematically for that learning if the full potential for leadership development through community is to be realized.

We begin our discussion with the content curriculum and a look at the changing nature of educational administration programs—the criticisms, challenges, and current directions moving us toward a more collaborative orientation. We then place this contextual overview within the framework of curriculum theory and the process curriculum. We conclude with practical suggestions for curriculum and instructional approaches that might be employed within learning community settings. We turn our attention first to the content curriculum, with a look at the current status of educational administration programs.

CONTENT CURRICULUM

"A disturbing and dangerous mismatch exists between what American society needs of higher education and what it is receiving" (Wingspread Group in Higher Eduction, 1993, p. 1). There is no shortage of critics willing to tell the higher education community what is wrong with preparation programs for teachers, principals, or superintendents. "Clearly the immediate task of our nation is to make certain that principals are competent for the changing school; that the new conditions facing school leaders are connected to redesigned programs for their preparation and certification. Today, those connections are incidental, even misaligned" (National Commission for the Principalship, 1990, p. 9).

Where Have We Been?

Murphy (1993) documents the inadequacy of the knowledge base in educational administration as it has existed in the past. He points to the indiscriminate adoption of practices, serious fragmentation of curricula, separation of practice and theory, a neglect of ethics, and lack of program accountability as some of the problems in a profession that "appears to enjoy the study of administration for its own sake" (Evans, in Murphy, 1992, p. 85). Murphy contends that preparation programs in general not only are not addressing the right issues, but also are doing a relatively poor job of addressing those they have chosen to address. Brent and Haller (1998) remind us again of those deficiencies in their work on benefits or the lack thereof of educational administration programs.

Given this state of the knowledge base, it is no wonder that critics have attacked everything from course content to a lack of connection to the practice of administration. "Most administrators receive fragmented overlapping, and often useless courses that add up to little" (Cooper & Boyd, in Murphy, 1993, p. 87).

Critics abound. Yet, experts in the field of educational administration have, until recently, been unable to come to agreement on what knowledge is of most worth. What should be included in the curriculum for the preparation of school leaders? What should future school leaders know and be able to do? There has been an inability or an unwillingness of faculty in educational administration programs to engage in serious curriculum development work. Therefore, in subtle and perhaps not so subtle ways, others' traditions or construction of what is important to know or do, seems to have been incorporated into university curricula. Democratic educators live with the dichotomy of attempting to make learning meaningful while attending to knowledge and skills expected by powerful political forces with interests that are anything but democratic (Apple & Beane, 1995). The need for change in preparation programs is apparent. Recent movements toward development of standards for preparation programs appear to be a possible answer.

Where Are We Now?

Most states have developed a set of standards for school leaders. Certification in those states typically is tied to students meeting those standards through university preparation programs or some type of portfolio demonstration of skills. Certification in one state does not ensure that one has met standards required for certification in another state. To further add to the confusion, several educational organizations have put forth standards and skills that they believe form the foundation of leadership behavior. The National Association of Elementary Principals, the American Association of School Administrators, the National Policy Board for Educational Administration (NPBEA), and the Council of Chief State School Officers (CCSSO) all have come forward with positions on this issue. It appears at this time that the various professional groups have come together to support the work of the NPBEA and it, in turn, has decided to work with the CCSSO, whose participants developed the Interstate School Leaders Licensure Consortium (ISLLC) standards for school leaders. While the ISLLC standards and the NPBEA's NCATE Curriculum Guidelines were developed by different groups, it was the primary goal of the organizations to maintain congruence between the two products as indicators for the licensing of principals and other school leaders for admission to practice.

The development of standards was in response to both groups' concern that a lack of professional structure would weaken the field of educational leadership. Although the ISLLC standards were developed primarily as a framework for "matters on learning and teaching and the creation of powerful learning environments" (Council of Chief State School Officers, 1996, p. 8), in many programs both the NCATE and the ISLLC standards are being used to guide not only preparation but licensure as well.

The issue of standards for the preparation of school leaders has received much attention of late. In response to poor test scores of students in public education, critics keep pointing the finger upward to universities and to the preparation of teachers and principals. Add to that discussion a perceived shortage of qualified candidates in both fields, and the issue of "what are universities doing?" receives extra attention. Thus the conversation is happening at local program levels as well as at state and federal levels. Federal grants are available for the renewal or restructuring of preparation programs. Private foundations such as Eli Broad and the Gates Foundations are making principal and superintendent preparation a priority; large school districts (such as the San Diego Unified School District) are starting their own preparation academies; districts are buying into Internet principal development programs.

The intent of the ISLLC standards was to present "a common core of knowledge, dispositions and performances that will help link leadership more forcefully to productive schools and enhanced educational outcomes" (Council of Chief State School Officers, 1996, p. 4). We believe the group has achieved that goal.

The ISLLC standards focus on developing leaders who facilitate the development of a shared vision; advocate, nurture, and sustain a school culture; ensure management of the operation; collaborate with families and community; act with integrity and fairness and in an ethical manner; and understand, respond to, and influence the broader political, social, and cultural context. NCATE advocates leadership studies in the areas of strategic leadership, instructional leadership, organizational leadership, and political and community leadership. We believe that the ISLLC and the NCATE standards are current, are tied to relevant literature on the subject, and can well serve as the foundation of the knowledge base in educational leadership programs, as they are in many states.

A closer look at a few NCATE and ISLLC standards demonstrates the link each has to a curriculum that fosters the development of learning communities. NCATE's Area I seeks to develop a strategic leader who, with others, can generate a vision and purpose, frame problems, achieve common goals and act ethically, influence institutional culture, and affirm core beliefs. NCATE's Area II emphasizes teaching leaders to develop learner-centered cultures and apply adult learning strategies to professional development. Area III prepares school leaders to use appropriate interpersonal skills to exhibit sensitivity, show respect and interest, and exhibit consistency and trustworthiness in improving the organization. ISLLC's Standard 1 supports the need for educational leaders who facilitate the development, articulation, implementation, and stewardship of a vision of learning that is supported and shared by the school community. ISLLC's Standard 2 advocates leaders who nurture and sustain a school culture and instructional program conducive to student learning and staff professional growth. The NPBEA knowledge and skill base for school leaders also advocates areas that would reinforce the work of leaders in developing learning communities. Domain 8, for instance, deals with instruction and the learning environment. It demands that leaders create school cultures for learning by possessing a substantial knowledge base and knowing how to plan, implement, and evaluate instructional programs collaboratively.

Standards, whether those of the ISLLC, NCATE, or NPBEA, should be used as a foundation in the development of programs in educational administration. The preparation and continuing development of school leaders is serious business, and the assessment of those leaders is a daunting task. There is some evidence (Coleman, 2000) that would suggest that the ISLLC standards do not have a high degree of validity or reliability. It is the responsibility of those in charge of preparation programs to ensure that what we are using as the foundation of our programs has legitimacy. The question that remains to be answered is whether we have the will to put any standards in place.

Where Should We Go?

If we are to use standards to guide how we do business in programs of educational administration, Ashby (2000) offers us a few strategies to improve the process and hopefully the end product:

1. Professional organizations need to be explicit and single voiced about the purpose of standards.
2. Programs need to explain how the standards address the needs for "creating learning environments, aligning curriculum, instruction and assessment" (p. 6) all through opportunities for lifelong learning and the building of networks.
3. Professional organizations, especially those focused on the work of the professorate, should educate professors on the importance of modeling and being systematic about what they do and what is expected of students as future school leaders.
4. Programs of educational administration should develop visions that are integrated with state and national standards; develop clear expectations for professional performance of their students; and help students find appropriate leadership roles at different times in their careers.
5. Preparation programs should use the standards as "a lens through

which to develop, promote, and assess professional development of professors teaching in educational administration preparation programs" (p. 6).

Furthermore, Ashby (2000) suggests that professional organizations and universities should support full-time internship experiences for future school leaders. Finally, she questions whether the higher education community will

> use the standards issue to point fingers, divide up turf, increase regulations, and play power politics, or will it use the standards issue as a means of developing a vertical learning community focused on the needs of our collective students—that is, focused on learning and the climate that supports learning for children and adults? (p. 3)

Certainly this is a thoughtful challenge to the profession.

We need to remember that the type of "knowledge needed to act competently as a principal relies more on the capacity to grasp meaning (a hermeneutic activity) than it relies on the possession of an abstract body of empirically derived skills and knowledge" (Evans, in Murphy, 1992, p. 7). We believe a process curriculum focusing on adult theory and constructivist ideals will have a great impact on the development of communities of learners who will in turn develop communities of learners in their schools or districts.

PROCESS CURRICULUM

Educational administration faculty have only begun to understand the potential of learning communities as vehicles for the development of transformational leaders, but we believe programs that prepare educational leaders using such a model have a tremendous advantage over traditional preparation approaches in this regard. We begin this discussion with some overarching guiding theoretical principles that we feel provide a conceptual base for the direction we will take. A look at individual and group development serves as a platform for the development of a variety of methods and strategies used in building community. The role of the professor in this process is also addressed. Then, as we consider activities to further both process and content curriculum, we make note of not only how learning communities operate effectively as cohesive groups, but also how they, in turn, promote the enhancement of individuals. Being a member of a developing learning community becomes the lesson.

Adult Learning Theory

Theories of adult learning and development must serve as a theoretical foundation for the creation of learning communities in educational administration programs. In cohesive groups where learning is problem-based and student-centered, academic learning is greatly enhanced (Knowles, 1985). Literature in adult education indicates that adults learn best when they can direct their own learning, influence decision making, focus on problems relevant to practice, tap their rich experiential backgrounds, and build strong relationships with peers (Merriam & Caffarella, 1991). Adult learners need to grow and learn with others, to feel less isolated in their learning, and to count on others as resources in their learning. Adult learners also need to have some control over the content of the learning experiences as well as the communities' decision-making processes (Barnett & Muse, 1993). The ability to influence the activities and topics of discussion, participate in the decision-making process (Knowles, 1980), develop goals, implement activities, and evaluate outcomes (Knowles, 1980) all positively contribute to an adult's sense of ownership and commitment to learning (Barnett & Muse, 1993).

Constructivism

The constructivist approach to teaching is based on research about how people learn. This theoretical frame also provides a conceptual base for the development of learning communities. Researchers suggest that each individual constructs knowledge instead of receiving it from others (Dewey, 1938; Piaget, 1970; Vygotsky, 1978). It is an active process that promotes thinking and reasoning (McBrien & Brandt, 1997). Consistent with the teachings of humanistic educators, "education should be a drawing forth of human potential rather than a handing down of pre-selected facts and skills" (Miller, 1990, p. 2). Adults should not be asked to conform to a model of knowing but rather to be involved in more of a discovery model where they are afforded opportunities to explore and test many alternative views (Levine, 1989; Norris & Barnett, 1994). Brooks and Grennon (1999) advocate that practices considered constructivist would include ideas such as teachers seeking and considering students' points of view; lessons orchestrated to challenge students' suppositions; relevant curriculum; lessons planned around big ideas; and students' learning assessed in the context of the learning environment. Because constructing knowledge requires trial and error, it necessitates an environment that encourages and supports risk taking. It also changes the power relationship between teachers and learners. Constructivism "empowers the learner and sees the construction of knowledge as requiring not only individual reflection, but interaction with others" (Wilson, 1993, p. 223). (Closely related to this concept is our discussion of ways to enhance the ethic of care, addressed in Chapter 4.)

Other Contemporary Views

Other curriculum views complement and extend the constructivist point of view regarding acquisition of knowledge. The cognitive view examines the complexities of context, the role of people and their feelings, and the interactive relationship between thinking and action (Wilson, 1993). Post-structuralism is values-driven, embraces the goal of equity, and believes that school leaders and the school community are the vehicles for achieving this goal. Leadership becomes a transformational, moral activity designed to overcome the bureaucratic demands that enable the status quo. Critical educators advocate an interdisciplinary approach to curriculum in order to create a democratic society. They empower individuals and celebrate differences. Teachers engage in critical inquiry that informs curriculum development (Wilson, 1993). What all these views have in common is a radically different approach to thinking about teaching and learning that must prevail if preparation programs are going to be successful in the future.

Using adult learning concepts and these contemporary views of curriculum as underpinnings, we advocate a process curriculum that consists of developing the individual as well as enhancing the process of group development. The need for both is examined here. (See Chapters 1 and 4 for a detailed discussion of transformational leadership development and enhancement of the ethic of care. Both concepts center around this methodology.)

Individual Development

In developing and maintaining learning communities, care must be taken to ensure that group processes assist individual members in realizing their potential. Henderson and Hawthorne (1995) use the term *emancipatory constructivism* to describe a curriculum approach that focuses on personal, social, and transpersonal liberation. In the personal liberation phase they emphasize the need to consider cultivation of an individual's "self-worth, identity, authenticity and self actualization during the learning process" (p. 5). This is also the foundation for the growth of the individual found in the humanistic curriculum that encompasses the concepts of individual meaning, freedom, integrity, and autonomy. When self-actualization and personal meaning are emphasized, individuals will develop into interdependent learning community members.

Drucker (1999) reminds us that knowledge workers of the future will have to know how to manage themselves, and that can be accomplished only by answering questions about oneself such as: "Who am I? What are my strengths? How do I work? Where do I belong? What is my contribution?" (p. 164). Buckingham and Coffman (1999) encourage leaders to use feedback tools to increase their understanding of who they are and how others perceive them. Kouzes and Posner (1987) draw a direct parallel between self-understanding and leadership. Self-understanding fosters a personal faith in one's capabilities, values, and convictions. Rogers (1969) noted that educational environments should promote self-discovery and exploration, and a deep respect for human life. Throughout the learning process, individuals must balance the realization of the community's purpose with the achievement and satisfaction of meeting personal goals (Yerkes, Norris, Basom, & Barnett, 1994). An assumption that permeates process curriculum in educational leadership programs, then, is the need for individuals to become reflective, to have increased sensitivity to and skill in understanding both the self and the community.

Group Development

When individuals within groups interact and become cohesive, groups develop into interdependent entities. Within such groups, individuals support each other, pool their resources, combine their efforts, and develop friendship bonds, rules, and rituals (Johnson & Johnson, 1987), forming the bases of a true learning community. The group needs to be guided in identifying concerns, gathering and analyzing data about its own beliefs and function, engaging in problem solving and action planning, and critically assessing the overt and covert meaning of its organizational life (Henderson & Hawthorne, 1995). Bonding together to achieve a greater purpose is the professed curriculum of the social reconstructionist. Emphasis is placed on learning that is relevant to the individual but not at the expense of the community (McNeil, 1985). Early efforts by Dewey (1938) to build democratic schools are visible in this process. As Patterson (in Apple & Beane, 1995) noted, education in a democratic society is characterized by shared interests, freedom to interact, participation, and relationships. Those involved in democratic schools see themselves as participants in communities of learners willing to give up the passive role of knowledge consumer and assume the active role of being involved in creating meaning through a curriculum that supports democratic experiences (Apple & Beane, 1995). Such a curriculum expands student involvement through integrating human skills, interaction skills, analytical and critical skills, as well as problem-solving skills. Culture in the learning community then develops a spiritual commitment that is expressed through a shared "pedagogical covenant." At this point, "the quality of life within the community and the quality of doing curriculum become one" (Henderson & Hawthorne, 1995, p. 98). This curriculum greatly enhances the opportunities for students to develop their personal dream, which will form the basis of their visions as school leaders.

Characteristics of learning communities include cohesiveness and social interactions among community members. Social interaction is an important component of human beings' genetic makeup (Brilhart & Galanes, 1992), and thus community members' attitudes, behaviors, and perceptions are likely to be influenced by those social interactions. Those interactions also allow members to influence the activities and topics of discussion, participate in the decision-making process, develop goals, and evaluate outcomes for their community. When such activities take place in a climate of mutual support and respect, they allow for collegial sharing that enhances ownership in community purpose. A humanistic curriculum (McNeil, 1985) and adult learning theory (Merriam & Caffarella, 1991) support individuals having the ability to reflect on their accumulating experiences to evaluate their own learning. Social reconstructionists (McNeil, 1985) applaud individuals' abilities to have a voice in the direction of the learning, become active participants in their own learning, trust their own capabilities, and depend on one another rather than just on an instructor for guidance and assistance.

We turn our attention now to a discussion of the central role played by the university professor and the instructional methods that might be used in supporting these conceptual approaches.

ROLE OF THE PROFESSOR

Preparation programs designed to prepare tomorrow's leaders will have to employ dramatically different instructional strategies than the lecture approach used to date in most programs (Johnson, Johnson, & Smith, 1991; Murphy, 1992). In a review of five major university programs in educational administration concerned with better preparing school leaders, Milstein and Associates (1993) found that the delivery of academic content needed to change in order to increase the potential for student learning.

Emerging literature on cohorts as learning communities focuses largely on the effects these communities have on students; however, there is also some indication of the impact on faculty (Barnett & Muse, 1993; Yerkes et al., 1994). Some professors are being forced to alter their preferred instructional strategies in order to pay attention to the needs of adult learners and use different methodologies. Although the debate continues as to the most appropriate role for instructors, many would argue that rather than being purveyors of knowledge, as they have been expected to be in the past, instructors need to be facilitators of learning in others (Merriam & Caffarella, 1991; Murphy, 1990, 1992; Yerkes et al., 1994). If instructors facilitate more student-centered discussions, then those students will be more willing to share information and will find their discussions more relevant to their real-world situations (Barnett & Muse, 1993).

Teaching or facilitating in a learning community requires that instructors use many different approaches. There will always be a place for didactic, teacher-centered learning. Clearly there are times when lectures or demonstrations are appropriate since it remains the purview of instructors to ensure that students are exposed to the knowledge base of educational administration. For the most part, however, a dedication to adult learning theory and the constructivist approach would dictate that students be more involved in learning than is typically expected in a didactic presentation. A balance of instructional approaches is needed, but overall the instructional program should "stress 'doing' rather than passive listening" (Griffiths, 1977, p. 433).

Facilitators using adult education theory understand that it is important to develop an open learning climate where social interaction is encouraged. An authoritarian tone on the part of the facilitator can stifle interaction, while a supportive climate of respect, openness, and acceptance can facilitate quality interaction (Forsyth, 1990). We agree with Merriam and Cafferella (1991) that an important part of the facilitator's role is to allow group members to feel important and worthwhile, have a sense of belonging, and be accepted by other group members. And, as Murphy (1992) contends, instruction in educational administration programs needs to become less generic and more personalized.

In developing learning communities facilitators become associated with students inside as well as outside the formal classroom setting. Since much time is spent on reflective seminars, social gatherings, "get to know me" activities, and individual conferences, professors get to know students much better than in typical courses and thus their relationships tend to be more personal than in traditional classes. Better relations between faculty and students can improve mentoring and advising, collaborative research opportunities, and long-term professional links. This relationship also allows faculty to better recognize students' abilities and skills and is helpful in developing individual talent as well as creating a situation for strong student recommendations for future administrative positions. At times, however, because of the closer relationships that evolve in learning communities, professors and students are privy to sensitive personal issues such as illnesses, family difficulties, and marital problems. Professors may be unaccustomed to dealing with intense personal issues and feel unqualified to provide support and counseling, while students may feel uncomfortable with the shift in traditional teacher–student roles (Basom, Yerkes, Norris, & Barnett, 1996). There are no easy answers to such dilemmas. However, a learning community provides a safe, risk-free environment where students and faculty alike can discuss and deal with such issues—a prime example of where the learning community becomes the lesson.

Professors also face other challenges and opportunities as they attempt to develop learning communities. Significant challenges may arise over issues such as course content and sequencing; instructional delivery; relationships between field experience and classes; involvement of practitioners in the program; entrance requirements; course requirements; and assessment (Basom et al., 1996). On the other hand, there are several benefits to faculty. As they grapple with the issues, professors begin to operate as their own learning community, growing professionally as new ideas are explored, tested, and revised. Collaboration and sharing, not frequently modeled in higher education programs, become the norm, with the potential of leading to stronger professional links with colleagues in the program as well as with colleagues in similar programs at other universities (Milstein & Associates, 1993). Professors also might find themselves more engaged in collaborative research of mutual interest with colleagues in other programs (Yerkes et al., 1994). As an example, in the epilogue to this book, we address this notion as we share our journey in the book's development.

Another factor that facilitators of learning communities need to address is the size of the group. Group size influences group interaction as well as the frequency and intensity of group interactions. Frequent interaction promotes positive involvement and accountability among members in accomplishment of group tasks (Johnson & Johnson, 1987). Educational leadership cohorts or learning communities typically range from 10 to 30 students. Research suggests 25 as the optimal size for allowing students to develop closer relationships with their peers, and for faculty to attend to the needs of individual students (Barnett & Muse, 1993).

INSTRUCTIONAL METHODS

We begin the discussion of instructional methods for developing learning communities by looking at several global methodologies, such as student voice, authentic assessment, and a focus on reflection. We then address more specific instructional methods, such as getting acquainted activities, problem-based learning, growth plans, portfolios, platforms, journals, and so on.

Student Voice

"Since democracy involves the informed consent of people, a democratic curriculum emphasizes access to a wide range of information and the right of those of varied opinions to have their viewpoint heard" (Apple & Beane, 1995, p. 13). Choice is an important factor in individual growth and adult development (Merriam & Caffarella, 1991). Students come from different perspective. How they like to learn, what they like to read, and what types of activities or projects best suit their learning style become important issues in their personal development. Students need to be given the freedom to construct their own learning, as the constructivists (Brooks & Grennon, 1999) suggest, by having a say in what and how they learn.

Students can be given responsibility for development of course outcomes, course requirements, schedules, grading, and other pieces of the course structure. In many learning communities, professors set guidelines or perimeters for student involvement and learning standards, then allow students to determine the most appropriate strategies or activities to use in achieving those standards. Students can be encouraged to become members of standing committees that make programmatic decisions, such as assigning students to mentors and organizing social activities (Barnett & Muse, 1993). These activities give students some control over their own learning as opposed to the feeling that the professor is dictating all the requirements.

Authentic Assessment

As we all know, there is far more to assessment than giving students grades. Assessment should be meaningful and authentic (Johnson & Johnson, 1996), measure what was learned as opposed to what was taught, and be based on knowledge and skills that focus on problems of practice (Tucker & Codding, 1998). Students should be involved in formulating learning goals (Merriam & Caffarella, 1991), choosing paths for achieving those goals, assessing their progress and success (Apple & Beane, 1995), planning how to improve, and implementing their plans. Educational administration programs use such ideas as student journals, problem-based learning activities, portfolio demonstrations, case scenarios, solving real-life problems of practice during internships, self-assessment of course performance objectives, and student–faculty interviews.

Focus on Reflection

School leaders should use reflective thinking to explore the complexities of schooling by evaluating and challenging existing practices within the school culture (Short & Twale, 1994). Reflecting on one's educational practice is seen as a necessary element for professional growth and can lead to greater probability of transfer, which we discuss further in Chapter 6. The process requires "establishing time for considering one's practice, committing to objectively and occasionally dealing with discomfort, all for the purpose of generating greater self awareness" (Hill, n.d., p. 1). Reflection on practice also "symbolizes the development of a locus of control" (p. 1) and stimulates a spiral of empowerment by moving students through describing what they presently do to reconstructing their practice for improvement. Whereas Schön (1983) focuses his work mainly on reflection of practice by individuals, Starratt (1995) encourages us to remember that "our understanding of leadership and change has deepened to the point where we realize that reflection has to take place with others more often than by oneself" (p. 67). Starratt encourages leaders therefore to invite the whole school community to reflect on what they are doing, with the goal of developing a reflective community. This notion of a reflective community is at the heart of a learning community.

Programs in educational administration need to explore methods to systematically assist students in becoming more reflective both individually and as part of the reflective learning community. We need to get better at both teaching and measuring reflection (Kerrins & Cushing, 1997). The humanistic and social reconstructionist approaches to curriculum support reflection that enhances individuals' abilities to question in a nonthreatening manner and thus foster a relevant and safe learning experience (McNeil, 1985). These experiences, in turn, enable students to develop support, build a trusting environment, and further clarify their personal vision or dream. Weekly or monthly reflective seminars provide opportunities for learners to diagnose, analyze, and reflect on their field-based experiences. During these seminars, students are encouraged to bring real-world experiences and problems to the group. Students are encouraged to "examine relationships, develop insights, and create personal meaning from their experiences" (Barnett & Muse, 1993, p. 405). (See Chapter 6 for further discussion on the importance of reflection in the transfer process.)

Trust-Building Activities

Early interactions among students allow them to share their values, beliefs, and expectations for joining the group. Some program faculty purposely structure initial activities to help stimulate meaningful social interactions. For instance, residential retreats are excellent settings for initiating a preparation program because students are allowed to engage in intense discussions about their values, aspirations, and expectations prior to beginning the formal preparation program. Other less costly and less time-consuming activities include participating in outdoor education programs such as "ropes courses," where students engage in team-building activities that can be successfully completed only with physical and emotional support from community members. These activities encourage students to understand and appreciate their colleagues' attitudes, skills, and aspirations so that a strong foundation of trust, upon which future social interactions can be built, is established early on (Barnett & Muse, 1993). These activities also build the strong collegial bonds that encourage long-term personal and professional networks.

Self-Discovery

Milstein and Associates (1993) remind us that "the more community members understand themselves, the more clearly they will understand and identify with their core beliefs, leadership styles and decision-making biases" (p. 155). A variety of self-assessment instruments can be used in developing the individual as a community member. Students can take inventories such as the Myers–Briggs Type Indicator, Gregoric Styles' assessment, the Leadership Profile Instrument (Kouzes & Posner, 1990), the KOLB Learning Styles Inventory, Tracom's (1981) Styles Awareness Training, FIRO-B, and/or McGregor's Diagnostic Inventory. Assessment feedback from the National Association of Secondary School Principals' Assessment Center Process, or the National Elementary School Principals' Administrative Diagnostic Inventory also can be used effectively for the purpose of helping students gain valuable information about their beliefs, skills, interests, and abilities that will help them develop individually and thus become better able to function as effective members of a community of learners.

Individual Growth Plans

Once students have used a variety of assessment instruments to evaluate themselves, they are encouraged to develop individual growth plans based on those assessment data. If assessment feedback is received from others in work situations, it adds a more realistic dimension for the students. Since perception is in the eye of the beholder, students should get as much feedback as possible before setting out to develop a growth plan based on not only what they feel are their strengths and weaknesses but also what others who work with them believe as well. Growth plans help individuals understand that effective leadership starts with looking at the self. Blumberg (1989) suggests that we are our primary tool in the craft of leadership and that "if we know that tool well—its blind spots, its sore points, its biases, its dreams—we can deal with the matter in front of us with a minimum of unintended distortions" (p. 18).

Platforms

Sergiovanni and Starratt (1979) introduced us to the idea of identifying a series of assumptions or beliefs, attitudes, and values that are the underpinnings of one's behavior as an educator. These statements form an individual's platform. Argyris and Schön (1974) refer to these as individuals' espoused theories of action, detailing the set of beliefs, values, and assumptions underlying their behavior. This belief system is referred to by Rokeach (in Henderson & Hawthorne, 1995) as a "framework made up of layers of beliefs with those at the core being the most firmly held and the least likely to be changed" (p. 95). Students are asked to develop platforms as they begin their program of study. In these platforms students should identify nonnegotiable (least likely to change) core values that are at the heart of who they are as moral leaders. All work, activities, and directions henceforth should constantly be assessed against this personal constitution. Over time one should be able to see these values manifested in the schools led by these students. Chapter 3 gives a good description of such a process through several case studies of students' platforms.

Portfolios

Portfolios are used in many educational administration programs as a form of authentic assessment. As an authentic assessment tool, the portfolio allows the student to provide firsthand documentation/proof of performance and contributions. Second, it allows for nearly unlimited flexibility and creativity. Documentation of performance and contributions can take many forms and numerous formats, including computer disks, CD ROMs, videotapes, and so on. Third, portfolio assessment provides a solid data and information base that can be used by students as the take-off point for continuous professional growth and development. Portfolios used in educational administration programs typically serve as assessments of student progress toward having met program outcomes or state standards for accreditation in the area of school leadership.

Apart from being used as an assessment tool for program purposes, the portfolio can serve the needs of individual students to (1) document continuous professional development; (2) reflect on past performances and conduct self-assessments at any time; (3) identify professional growth goals and plan for learning opportunities or other jobs; and (4) provide concrete documentation of leadership performance and leadership accomplishments. In other words, it provides the student with an opportunity to reflect on his or her performance, job satisfaction, and life purpose, and to consciously choose how to change course if needed (Schwahn, 1998). (See Chapter 6 for further discussion on the importance of portfolios in the transfer process.)

Problem-Based Learning Activities

Problem-based learning is an approach that had its origin in the field of medicine. At the center of each project is a problematic situation that students are likely to encounter when they become school leaders (Bridges & Hallinger, 1997). The process takes problems from the complex realities of school and engages learners in acquiring new knowledge to collaboratively solve the problems. Each project culminates with a product and/or a performance that resembles the way the problem would have been dealt with in the world of practice. "Students do not merely write or talk about what they would do to resolve the problem. Instead, they collectively decide on a course of action, implement their decision, and experience the consequences of their actions" (Bridges & Hallinger, 1997, p. 133).

Journals

Journals help students learn about themselves, document the happenings in their learning experiences, and put individual and group growth in perspective. The most important reason to keep a journal is to learn about oneself. To learn from experiences, we must think about the things we observe, then use these observations to learn more about ourselves. By writing in a journal, we replay our roles in the events of the day and pose questions about those learnings that may lead to other learnings. If done correctly, this exercise gives students a chance to study their own behavior and emotions. Keeping a journal is especially beneficial for those who are not naturally curious or contemplative, but also serves well those who are contemplative by providing an outlet to recall things learned (Peck, n.d.). (See Chapter 6 for further discussion on the important role of journals as a tool to reinforce the transfer process.)

Cooperative-Learning Activities

Tasks that require the sharing of skills and resources foster the habit of collaboration and mutual support (Johnson & Johnson, 1987). Group projects such as the development of a group mission, group norms, and behavioral expectations are recommended during the beginning development stage of a learning community to help build support and cohesiveness, which will lead to easier achievement of individual and group needs. "Communities of learners in democratic schools are marked by an emphasis on cooperation and collaboration rather than on competition. People see their stake in others, and arrangements are created that encourage young people to improve life of the community by helping others" (Apple & Beane, 1995, p. 11). If college classrooms stress and reward cooperation, students will respond cooperatively, and a sense of community will result (Johnson, Johnson, & Smith, 1991).

Social Gatherings

Opportunities for students to meet over dinner, commute together, plan group meals, organize social events with group facilitators, and conduct celebrations of personal milestones, completion of classes, and graduation are all activities that also will provide for the development of social interactions within the learning community. Social directors for the class period can be designated to foster such outings.

Getting-Acquainted Activities

Time must be systematically allotted during each class period for students to get to know one another better. These activities might include having one student pick a topic of the day that all students need to talk about in round-robin fashion. The goal is self-disclosure; students on a daily or weekly basis learn a little bit more about one another.

SUMMARY

States and university programs need to embrace standards that can be used as a foundation in the development of programs in educational administration. Also, we believe that professors in those programs need to change how learning is facilitated. Only then can we begin to take seriously the business of developing learning communities within the university class environment that will lead students to want to model those same skills in their work as school leaders. Only then can we hope to see the transfer of knowledge, dispositions, and skills from the university classroom to the workplace of students.

Ashby (2000) sums up the work to be accomplished in educational leadership programs. She contends that programs should be (1) creating learning environments and (2) aligning curriculum, instruction, and assessment. Regardless of the standards used to guide educational administration curricula, we believe that using appropriate content through a process curriculum will enhance the development of strong learning communities. We agree with Milstein and Associates (1993) that this process provides

> the model of how schools can be transformed into adult learning communities. Cohort members who share in this powerful experience recognize how this unique learning approach can be transferred to the school site. They have experienced empowerment as adult learners and are more aware of the need to practice collaborative leadership as school administrators. (p. 201)

6

The Legacy of Learning Communities:
Transfer to the Workplace

A MAJOR PREMISE of our model of learning communities is that educational leaders must be able to apply their leadership preparation experiences in school settings. Application assumes not only that leaders' actions change, but also that their dispositions and knowledge are affected. These dispositions and knowledge, in the form of altered or reinforced values, determine the quality of leaders' performance (see Chapter 1 for a discussion of these value orientations). Our contention is that those of us who bear the responsibility for preparing future leaders must consciously assist these leaders to develop the values, skills, and knowledge needed to fulfill their roles. This goal is clearly the legacy of educational leadership preparation cohort programs (Norris, Barnett, Basom, & Yerkes, 1996).

How can such a challenging, yet important, legacy expect to be achieved? The answer to this critical question will be explored in this chapter. Our discussion centers on the importance of learning transfer, which is defined as the ability to repeat, modify, or generalize one's behavior from one situation to another (Detterman, 1993; Hunter, 1971). We agree with Bransford and Schwartz (1999), who contend that educators are deeply concerned about helping students apply or transfer their classroom experiences beyond the initial learning situation. The ultimate goal in transferring learning is to educate people, rather than merely train individuals to conduct various tasks (Broudy, 1977).

To examine transfer and its relevance in developing transformational leaders, we have organized the chapter into two major parts. First, we explore the underlying principles of the transfer process, including the rationale behind transfer and the major factors instructional designers should attend to when developing transfer strategies. The second part focuses on how educators can strive to apply the concepts of transfer in assisting aspiring school leaders to develop learning communities in their own work settings. Purposeful learning activities must be implemented for transfer to occur, rather than leaving application to the participants (Hunter, 1971; Ottoson, 1995). Our discussion reflects the conceptual background of leadership presented in Chapter 1, along with the model of learning communities introduced in Chapter 2. The chapter also addresses some of the challenges in creating learning communities as well as promising approaches instructors can use to encourage transfer in the workplace.

THE CONCEPT OF LEARNING TRANSFER

Learning transfer has deep philosophical roots, which have shaped some of our current educational practices. For instance, Plato's notion of continuity and the Buddhist scholars' writings about dependent origination were early attempts to understand the relationship between individuals' knowledge and their learning environments (Beach, 1999). These early philosophies suggested that individuals constantly strive to connect their knowledge with the social context of their lives. Based on these early principles, many of our current educational strategies, such as basic skills instruction, critical thinking skills, problem-based learning, and vocational education, are aimed at applying knowledge in a new setting or context (Beach, 1999; Bridges, 1992; Hunter, 1971).

Given educators' continuing interest in transfer, we believe a more thorough description of this concept is warranted. Therefore, we will examine what we know about transfer by describing the relevance of this concept and the major factors influencing transfer.

Transfer and Its Importance

Why has learning transfer consistently captured the attention of educators? Caffarella (in press) suggests three reasons for transfer being so important in today's educational environment. First, because employers are investing significant human and financial resources in professional development and training programs, they are interested in obtaining a return on their investment. They want to know that these programs are having an impact on their employees' skills as well as their organization's marketing programs and productivity. Second, as communities continue to struggle with complex social problems (e.g., drug abuse, violence, health care), city officials desire programs that can positively affect social agencies and ultimately the lives of their community members. Finally, the rapid pace of change in individuals' personal and professional lives constantly challenges them to consider new ways of behaving. Transfer, by its very nature, is about change and adaptation, a topic we will explore in the next section.

Despite the philosophical, intellectual, and practical appeal of learning transfer, some authors caution that there is a lack of empirical evidence supporting successful transfer. For instance, Detterman and Sternberg (1993) suggest:

> Most studies fail to find transfer. . . . [T]hose studies claiming transfer can only be said to have found transfer by the most generous of criteria and would not meet the classical definition of transfer. . . . In short, from studies that claim to show transfer and that don't show transfer, there is no evidence to contradict Thorndike's general conclusions: Transfer is rare, and its likelihood of occurrence is directly related to the similarity between two situations. (p. 15)

As a result of these spurious claims about the power of learning transfer, authors such as Broudy (1977) and Bransford and Schwartz (1999) are calling for new ways to conceptualize and measure transfer. While their ideas are important to further our understanding of the cognitive processes and practical applications of transfer, they are beyond the scope of our focus. What is important, we believe, is demonstrating the relationship between transfer and the change process, a topic to which we now turn our attention.

FACTORS AFFECTING TRANSFER AND CHANGE

Successful transfer must account for individuals' needs and preferences, the characteristics of the practice or innovation to be transferred, and the organizational context in which transfer is to occur. Marini and Genereux (1995) state it best.

> At one time or another the importance of each basic element of transfer—*task, learner,* and *context*—has been emphasized by educational theorists. Given that each element plays a key role in the transfer process, taking all three into account when designing instruction is most advisable. A trend in this direction, toward a more wholistic approach to achieving transfer, is apparent. (p. 5, emphasis added)

Therefore, a clear understanding of how individuals cope with change (the learner), what features of an innovation influence its transfer (the task), and the organizational factors affecting transfer (the context) is critical in determining how to transfer learning successfully from one situation to another. We will discuss each of these topics as they relate to learning transfer.

Personal Change and Reflection (the Learner)

Individuals' history with change can have a great impact on their willingness to transfer or apply their learning to other situations (Caffarella, in press). The change process, as Hall and Hord (1987) have discovered, involves a predictable series of developmental concerns. Typically, when individuals are confronted with a change or innovation, they develop self-concerns, focusing on their insecurity about being able to adapt. As these initial concerns diminish, management concerns arise, which reflect their capability to actually manage or administer the innovation. In the final developmental stage, impact concerns emerge, revealing individuals' desire to determine how the innovation is affecting other people and how to adapt it for future use.

Related to these views of personal change, is the notion of reflection or reflective practice. As Daudelin (1996) suggests, reflection is a way to draw inferences from experiences and to inform future practice, and has strong implications for learning transfer. In this sense, reflection is a process that allows individual learners to construct their own knowledge (see Chapter 5). Various writers have uncovered the elements constituting the reflective learning process, typically in the form of stages or levels of reflection. King and Kitchener (1994), for example, view reflection as a seven-stage process, ranging from pre-reflective thinking (three stages) to quasi-reflective thinking (two stages), to reflective thinking (two stages). Similarly, Sparks-Langer, Simmons, Pasch, Colton, and Starko (1990) have developed a reflective thinking framework, capturing various hierarchical levels of the language and thinking processes that humans use to integrate their experiences. According to their framework, the lowest levels of reflective thinking deal with simple descriptive language to describe thoughts and actions; however, theories, guiding principles, and/or ethical arguments are used in the higher levels of reflective thought.

Despite these attempts to capture various stages of reflection, perhaps the most well-known description of the reflective learning process is David Kolb's (1984) experiential learning theory. The power of Kolb's learning cycle is best advanced by Vince (1998).

> The popularity of the learning cycle arises in part from its accessibility to managers, both as a way of comprehending the processes of individual and organizational learning and development, and in terms of perceiving aspects of the process that may currently be omitted . . . . The learning cycle is an accessible way of expressing both the importance of experiential knowledge and the link between theory and practice. (p. 306)

Briefly, the theory suggests that learning occurs within a cycle "whereby knowledge is created through the transformation of experience" (Kolb, 1984, p. 26). The cycle comprises four phases, beginning with the concrete experience phase, which represents an event or situation individuals use as the basis for their learning. Typically, these events have happened in the past or to someone else, or, in some cases, may be occurring as the situation is taking place (what Donald Schön, 1983, calls "reflection in action"). In the second phase, reflective observation, individuals reexamine the event or situation by recalling its circumstances or context, asking such questions as: Who was involved? What happened? Has the event happened before? In this second phase of the reflective learning cycle, individuals gather facts about the situation in order to make informed judgments, which occur in the next phase, abstract conceptualization. During this third stage of the reflective process, individuals attempt to make sense of an event by drawing inferences, insights, and conclusions about their own and others' motives, as well as assessing why the situation was handled well or poorly and what should occur in the future. The final phase, active experimentation, represents individuals' new or reinforced thoughts, feelings, and actions. Acting on the conclusions drawn from the event stimulates individuals to take a proactive role in their learning by experimenting with new ideas.

As active experimentation takes place, the learning cycle has come "full circle"; these actions become the concrete experiences for further reflection and refinement. In this way, Kolb's theory is seen as a dynamic and ongoing cyclical learning process where "individual[s] can manage [their] own learning through reflecting on experience and thereby be in control of self-development" (Vince, 1998, pp. 305–306). The explicit connection between these phases of reflection and transfer occurs in the active experimentation phase. During this stage of reflection, learners consider how to apply their insights by asking, "So what does this all mean, and how can what was learned be applicable to my situation?" (Caffarella, in press). In fact, some research suggests that the metacognitive processes of reflection are instrumental in successful transfer in science, math, computer programming, and literacy (Bransford & Schwartz, 1999). Therefore, as we will discuss later in the chapter, learning activities that promote reflective thinking are essential for learning transfer.

Features of the Innovation (the Task)

Learning transfer also is influenced by features of the innovation or the learning tasks that are expected to be transferred. Some of the early work on how innovations are diffused throughout an organization indicates there are important qualities of the innovation that ultimately affect its use. For instance, Rogers (1983) noted that the relative advantage, compatibility, observability, trialability, and complexity of an innovation greatly influenced its likelihood of being adopted. Therefore, if members of an organization do not view the change as being beneficial, sense that it is extremely complicated, and/or have difficulty observing it in practice, then the chances of the innovation being accepted and implemented are greatly reduced.

Other characteristics of an innovation that influence its transferability have been identified. The perceived similarity between two situations affects whether individuals can apply new knowledge and skills (Detterman & Sternberg, 1993; Hunter, 1971). The more similar the new situation is to the original learning environment, the more likely transfer will occur. Caffarella (in press) suggests that program planners must consider the content or substantive features of the innovation when designing learning activities that are meant to transfer this content into the workplace.

Organizational and Social Factors (the Context)

Besides individuals' personal experience with change and the features of the innovation itself, organizational and social factors can impede or facilitate the implementation of the innovation. Caffarella (in press) argues that an organization's culture (e.g., concrete support for continuous learning, previous history with change and innovation) can support or inhibit transfer. For instance, various internal conditions, especially material, human, and symbolic support, are essential for an innovation to be successfully implemented (Berman & McLaughlin, 1976). Perhaps the most critical of these is collegial support and interest, especially if tangible resources are required to sustain the change (Fleisher, 1985). Likewise, external factors, including social, economic, and political conditions, can affect the use of an innovation (Berman & McLaughlin, 1976; Caffarella, in press). For example, the termination of funding (Achilles, 1994) and changes in federal regulations and policies (White, 1990) have been found to impede the continuation of new programs.

Clearly, a growing number of economic and pragmatic factors are making learning transfer as important today as at any time in our history of educational program planning and delivery. Effective transfer, however, does not happen by accident. Program planners must be cognizant of the personal characteristics of learners, especially how they cope with change; the characteristics of the practice or innovation to be transferred; and the organizational and social context that supports or inhibits change efforts. How, then, can these principles guide program planners in attempting to assist educational leaders to build learning communities in their school settings? We now direct our attention to this crucial question.

TRANSFER AND LEARNING COMMUNITIES

In Chapters 1 and 3 we presented a conceptual framework of transformational leadership and its development. We emphasized the importance of providing a context for the acquisition and application of transformational dispositions, knowledge, and performance skills through a learning community experience. In other words, we described the means necessary for individuals to reach their goals by moving to higher levels of consciousness (see Chapter 1). In addition, our model of learning communities (see Figure 1.1) reflects the phases of growth and development individuals experience during a learning cohort (i.e., the inner triangle) and the transfer or application of these skills to a workplace setting (i.e., the outer triangle). Finally, we have described some of the essential instructional processes and content to be experienced in the learning cohort in Chapter 5. Therefore, our intention in the remainder of this chapter is to build on these previous concepts by discussing those processes that will encourage transfer from the cohort program to the real world of practice. In particular, we will stress how future educational leaders can develop learning communities that mirror many of the qualities of the cohort learning environment they experienced during their leadership preparation program.

To begin our discussion, we review what is known about transferring skills and knowledge from educational leadership preparation programs to schools. Earlier studies as well as our own research will be summarized. Next, we identify some of the pressing challenges and problems in transferring the knowledge and skills introduced in a learning cohort to educational settings. Finally, we conclude by examining practical ways in which instructors and facilitators can assist students to transfer the lessons learned about learning communities from the cohort program to their school organizations.

Transfer in Leadership Development Programs

Given the importance of change and the "belief [that] transfer lies at the heart of our educational system" (Bransford & Schwartz, 1999, p. 61), researchers and practitioners have attempted to determine the lasting effects on graduates of educational leadership preparation programs. Unfortunately, most of the news about the impact of preparation on subsequent performance is not promising. On the one hand, there has not been much empirical work focusing on leadership program impact. As Brent and Haller (1998) claim:

> The fact that an advanced degree is required to administer schools, however, tells little if anything about whether the credential is truly needed to produce a given set of outcomes. Indeed, why should we believe that the best way to become a good [school] administrator is to go to graduate school? Given the extensiveness of mandated preservice training and the potential magnitude of its cost, it is disheartening to discover that the efficacy of graduate training in educational administration is relatively unstudied. (p. 2)

On the other hand, when empirical data have been collected about the lasting effects of leadership preparation programs, the findings are less than encouraging. Not only do program graduates tend to dismiss the importance of their formal preparation (Goldman & Kempner, 1988; Schnur, 1989), but preparation programs also have not demonstrated much impact on their graduates' subsequent performance or on school improvement efforts (Brent, 1998; Haller, Brent, & McNamara, 1997). As has recently been reported:

> Graduate training in educational administration has no significant positive influence on school effectiveness .... If graduate training in school administration improves competence, then the principals of effective schools should, on average, be more highly trained than principals of less effective schools. This is not what we found. (Brent, 1998, p. 6)

Furthermore, when educational leadership professors have been asked to describe the benefits afforded to students in their programs, they tend to ignore possible effects on students' workplace performance. Rather, many professors comment on students' lasting interpersonal relationships and professional contacts (Hill, 1995; Milstein & Associates, 1993; Milstein & Krueger, 1993). For example, our comprehensive survey of educational leadership program faculty revealed that they were much more likely to report benefits to students experienced during their program of study, rather than after completing the program (Barnett, Basom, Yerkes, & Norris, 2000). Those few faculty who mentioned program impact beyond the university setting alluded to the "interpersonal relationships that developed among cohort members [and] professional contacts with school district personnel . . . , [which make] students more visible and marketable for future jobs" (Barnett et al., 2000, p. 271).

On the surface, these professors' reactions suggest that transfer appears to be of little importance or consequence in leadership preparation programs. However, we believe they have identified a crucial aspect of transfer needed for learning communities, namely, the importance of developing healthy and collaborative relationships. Without the formation of mutual trust, collegiality, and empowerment, transformational leaders will not be able to build a learning community. And as Starratt (1995) reminds us, forming and maintaining relationships are essential for creating a reflective community of learners.

Nevertheless, because our profession lacks the evidence to demonstrate learning transfer, some people are calling for more empirical studies (Barnett et al., 2000; Barnett & Muse, 1993; Brent & Haller, 1998). One example of this type of investigation was conducted by Leithwood, Jantzi, and Coffin (1995). Their study sought to obtain the perceptions of teachers about the leadership capabilities of graduates of various leadership preparation programs who were serving as principals or assistant principals. Their findings revealed that the cohort learning experience and prior mentoring with school administrators were related to leadership effectiveness. Although investigations of this sort have "formidable difficulties . . . , the importance of the topic requires more attention than it has [received]" (Brent & Haller, 1998, p. 2).

The Challenge of Developing Learning Communities

Besides the dearth of empirical evidence about transfer, there are additional challenges associated with attempts to transfer skills and knowledge about learning communities into the workplace. As we noted in Chapter 5, educational leadership cohorts can mirror a learning community by introducing the content and learning processes associated with transformational leadership. As they develop their personal dream, future educational leaders can envision how to develop learning communities in their own school organizations.

Transfer, we contend, is directly related to the personal change process and levels of concern described earlier. Because the transfer process affects leaders' dispositions and actions, both must be addressed in a formal program of study. Dispositions constitute the affective dimension of learning and are reflected in leaders' self-concerns. By exploring their personal values, beliefs, and preferences, leaders reduce their self-doubts and concerns, allowing them to consider how best to apply their actions in the work setting. Yet, as these new practices occur, management concerns arise such as: What is the best way to put these new practices in place? Who should be involved in developing and implementing these practices? Finally, impact concerns emerge as leaders consider how well these new practices are working for students and adults.

Taking these three levels of concern into account, transferring the skills and knowledge about learning communities to the workplace appears to be a straightforward process. While there are a host of instructional activities that instructors can use to promote transfer (which we will describe in more detail in the next section), there are three major dilemmas that pose difficulties for learning community transfer:

1. Individuals are asked to conduct transfer, yet learning communities require the commitment of large groups of people (Starratt, 1995).
2. Many differences exist between the original learning situation (i.e., the learning cohort) and the school organization where learning transfer is to occur.
3. Individuals have little control over many internal and external organizational forces, which can sabotage their efforts to develop a learning community.

We believe these challenges, while serious, can be overcome by transformational leaders who are committed to creating learning communities. To further explore these problems and how they can be addressed, we will first examine each challenge and then propose how school–university partnerships may be a possible remedy that educational leadership program planners, students, and district personnel can employ to help overcome these obstacles.

Individual Versus Group Application. Most experimental studies of transfer ask subjects to solve a new problem without the aid or assistance of other people or resources, often referred to as "sequestered problem solving" (Bransford & Schwartz, 1999). This same dilemma exists for members of an educational leadership cohort who are attempting to apply their knowledge about learning communities in their own organizations. In most cases, an individual is the only one from his or her school involved in the preparation program. Therefore, the individual lacks contact with colleagues who are being introduced to these ideas about how to develop learning communities. As a result, the degree of original learning in the cohort may not suffice for transfer (Bransford & Schwartz, 1999; Lee, 1998; Lee & Pennington, 1993), especially in establishing a learning community.

Furthermore, the complexity of a learning community makes transfer extremely difficult. Establishing and maintaining learning communities, as we have discussed earlier, requires complex organizational structures and interpersonal relationships. As Rogers (1983) claims, the more complex, the less visible, and the less compatible with current practice the innovation is, the more difficult it is to transfer or apply the innovation. Therefore, asking a single person to create a learning community poses a daunting task; however, empowered transformational leaders can help to create such environments.

Differences Between a Cohort and the Workplace. One of the guiding principles of transfer is recognizing the similarity between two learning situations. The more similar the two events, the greater the likelihood of positive transfer (Detterman & Sternberg, 1993; Hunter, 1971). Many differences exist between the learning experiences of a graduate education cohort and a school organization. As just mentioned, one significant difference is that individuals attend graduate programs, yet learning communities in school organizations require the involvement of large groups of people. Some of the additional structural and contextual differences between cohorts of graduate students and school organizations include the following:

- Cohort members typically engage in activities for substantial periods of time (e.g., retreats, weekend sessions, blocks of time each week). Members of school organizations rarely have the time to engage in such concentrated and sustained professional development opportunities. Teachers tend to be segregated from one another, and the demands of school life minimize opportunities for collective interaction (Little & McLaughlin, 1993). New models of staff development, however, emphasize the importance of collaborative efforts, such as whole-faculty study groups.
- Cohort members usually begin together and stay together for the duration of their graduate program. Because schools are dynamic organizations, turnover of teaching staff and administrators is much more common than in graduate cohort programs. Not only is it is uncommon for all teachers and administrators to begin their involvement in a school at the same time, but also they rarely remain in the same school together for significant time periods.
- School organizations are places of employment, whereas a graduate school cohort is a form of professional development. Governance, policy issues, and power can dominate school organizations. Principals and assistant principals evaluate teachers, which can have a bearing on their continued employment. Although professors certainly evaluate students in graduate cohorts, the stakes clearly are not as high as in the workplace. In addition, students tend to attend graduate education leadership programs by choice. In contrast, some teachers may be as-

signed to schools or classrooms against their will, making collaboration and community building difficult to achieve.

- Cohorts tend to be smaller in size than most school organizations. Many cohort programs enroll fewer than 25 students; however, most schools, especially secondary schools, employ far more teachers than the typical cohort. Because of the importance communication and trust play in developing learning communities, what may work in small graduate cohort programs may not always apply in larger, more complex school organizations.

Little Control over Internal and External Forces. Earlier we noted that change and innovation are influenced by various internal and external forces (Berman & McLaughlin, 1976; Caffarella, in press). Schools and their surrounding communities have cultures that may or may not be conducive to developing and sustaining a learning community. Each school organization has a unique history that can facilitate or impede the creation of a healthy learning community (Deal & Peterson, 1999). For instance, because a learning community requires high trust and collaboration, if competition, cliques, and divisiveness prevail, then a complete overhaul of the culture is necessary for a learning community to have any chance of surviving. As we know, cultures are not easy to change, even in the best of circumstances (Deal & Peterson, 1999; Fullan, 1993; Schein, 1992).

Ultimately, the problem faced by students in graduate programs is that often they do not have the power or authority to deal with these internal and external forces. Typically, they are teachers who have decided on their own to return to graduate school. The school or the district has no formal investment in their participation in the leadership preparation program. Arrangements may be made for students to work with the principal or other teachers in their school during their graduate program; however, these students still lack decision-making authority and are not held accountable for outcomes. Not until these students become formal leaders within the school organization will they have the power and influence necessary to shape learning communities.

What can be done to overcome some of these persistent differences between the realities of a learning cohort and a school as a learning community? The problems just noted indicate that individual graduate students are faced with the challenge of transferring complex knowledge and skills about learning communities into school organizations that may or may not be appropriate settings for such transfer. One possible solution to this dilemma is the formation of interorganizational partnerships between university preparation programs and schools and/or districts; in other words, the creation of an expanded learning community. Successful school–university partnerships not only establish operating procedures (e.g., selecting students, matching mentors with students), but also clarify program content and student learning expectations (Erlandson, Skrla, Westbrook, Hornback, & Mindiz-Melton, 1999; Fusarelli & Smith, 1999; Whitaker & Barnett, 1999). As universities and school districts develop a foundation of mutual trust and collaboration, the philosophy and practice of learning communities can become an intentional part of the curriculum and delivery process. Clearly, such partnerships will take time to develop (Trubowitz, 1986) and may require a more interdependent interorganizational arrangement, such as a collaborative or symbiotic partnership model (see Barnett, Hall, Berg, & Camarena, 1999).

Strategies for Encouraging Learning Communities

Besides working to establish collaborative partnerships between universities and school districts, learning communities can offer many promising instructional activities to promote transfer. We agree with Caffarella's (in press) assertion that program planners have more control over program design and content than do other factors, such as the organizational context in which transfer is to occur and community and societal forces affecting innovations. Therefore, it is to these design and delivery features that we now direct our attention. In particular, we will examine Caffarella's (in press) framework for transfer design, describe specific activities that promote transfer, and identify ways to assess the impact of transfer on individuals and organizations.

Framework for Transfer. Caffarella's framework for transfer provides a starting point for university faculty who are serious about assisting learners to transfer information from the instructional setting to their school settings. This three-part framework focuses on: (1) the appropriate timing of transfer activities; (2) considerations of the personal, contextual, and cultural factors affecting which transfer activities program planners might select; and (3) who is responsible for ensuring that transfer occurs. The first and last of these components will be briefly discussed here. The second element, instructional activities, will be examined in the next section.

Attention to transfer can occur before, during, or after the delivery of a leadership development program. For instance, when school–university partnerships are implemented, much preplanning needs to occur (Erlandson et al., 1999). In particular, decisions need to be made about how best to recruit participants, what adjustments in program content and delivery are appropriate, who will be involved in delivering the program, and what learning is expected to be transferred from the preparation program to the workplace. Some partnerships use a steering committee to oversee these types of activities (Whitaker & Barnett, 1999). Once the preparation program has begun, careful attention needs to be directed to aligning course content and practice in school settings. If mentors are used to assist aspiring school leaders, they need to be constantly apprised of the program content and how they can provide meaningful learning and support in the workplace. Finally, once programs have finished, ongoing follow-up activities can be implemented; however, only in rare cases do leadership preparation programs continue to work with their graduates as they enter the workforce. One promising way for universities to maintain their association with graduates is to become more involved in the formal induction programs many districts are instituting for new school administrators.

As suggested above, a variety of people are needed to ensure that the seeds of transfer have a chance of sprouting. Clear expectations about the roles and responsibilities of these people can be communicated from the very beginning of the leadership preparation program. Some of the key role providers in a leadership development program, especially when instituting a partnership, include: learners, university faculty, clinical faculty (i.e., individuals responsible for coordinating internships or on-site activities), mentors, and school district officials. While the support of key district officials (e.g., superintendent, personnel director, school board members) is essential for successful partnerships (Melaville, Blank, & Asayesh, 1993), those actually delivering and participating in the preparation program—instructors, learners, and mentors—need to coordinate learning activities aimed at transfer. Certainly, steering committees can provide some guidance about the overall operation of the partnership. Nevertheless, the day-to-day learning activities must be coordinated by those people actually delivering and participating in the preparation program (Hannay, 1994).

Promising Transfer Activities. We argued earlier in this chapter that transfer is directly related to the reflective learning process. Many proponents of reflection and transfer (e.g., Barnett & O'Mahony, n.d.; Caffarella, in press; Daudelin, 1996; Hole & McEntee, 1999) advocate the use of a variety of individual and group techniques for ensuring that learners apply information from one setting to another. Table 6.1 summarizes individual and group learning strategies available to program planners. In some instances, individual strategies are not performed in isolation, but involve

Table 6.1. Individual and Group Learning Activities That Promote Learning Transfer

Individual Strategies	*Group Strategies*
Individual learning plans	Transfer teams
Mentoring and coaching sessions	Follow-up
Job rotation/guided internships	Support groups
Journals and e-mail reflections	Networking
Portfolios	Training protocols
Reflective case records, projects	Action research
Critical incident protocols	
Electronic bulletin boards and chat rooms	

interactions with other people (e.g., mentoring/coaching, electronic bulletin boards, chat rooms).

When employing these individual and group learning activities, special attention should be given to the various phases of reflection noted earlier. Not only should learners be allowed to re-examine the context of a situation (concrete experience and reflective observation) and assess meaning (abstract conceptualization), but they also should have the opportunity to apply personal insights to their work setting (active experimentation). If learners are constantly pushed to explore the existing elements of their school culture that will either facilitate or inhibit transfer, they will be in a better position to capitalize on assets and avoid possible pitfalls in implementing new practices. Reflection, therefore, provides learners with a process for determining the means necessary to acquire their goals, a process we have argued is essential for raising consciousness to new levels and becoming transformational leaders.

Impact of Transfer. To ascertain the degree to which transfer is occurring in the workplace, professors and/or program planners must gather evidence from a variety of sources. Guskey and Sparks (1991) provide a useful framework, and guiding questions, for evaluating how professional development activities can affect participants. They propose five levels of impact:

1. Participants' reactions. Was time well spent? Did materials make sense? Was the environment conducive to learning?
2. Participants' learning. Were the intended knowledge and skills acquired?

3. Organization support and change. What was the impact on the organization? Was implementation advocated and supported?
4. Participants' use of new knowledge and skills. Were new skills and knowledge applied?
5. Student learning outcomes. Was student performance or achievement affected? Was students' physical or emotional well-being improved?

This framework is particularly appropriate for examining the impact of transfer at various levels because it accounts for: (a) individual learning (levels 1 and 2), (b) application (level 4), and (c) school organization (level 3) and student learning (level 5) effects. This multidimensional framework provides evidence about personal growth and application as well as organizational changes and constraints, all of which we have argued are important factors in determining the degree to which learning in the learning cohort has transferred to the workplace.

FINAL THOUGHTS ON TRANSFER

The views expressed in this chapter might suggest that any attempts to transfer knowledge and skills from a graduate cohort setting to the workplace are extremely difficult to achieve. Clearly, the challenges are daunting; however, interinstitutional agreements can begin to resolve some of the inherent difficulties in learning community transfer. In addition, thoughtful instructional design and delivery can encourage positive transfer.

Indeed, there is growing evidence that educational leadership cohort members experience what it means to be part of a learning community. For example, healthy interpersonal relationships are established (Barnett, Basom, Yerkes, & Norris, 2000; Basom, Yerkes, Norris, & Barnett, 1996; Norris, Barnett, Basom, & Yerkes, 1996; Norton, 1995; Yerkes, Basom, Barnett, & Norris, 1995), isolation is reduced and social bonding flourishes (Basom et al., 1996; Hill, 1995; Norris et al., 1996), common purpose increases (Leithwood et al., 1995), and a sense of self and personal dream develop (Norris, Basom, Yerkes, & Barnett, 1996). Claims have been made that cohort programs "build a pool of administrative-certified applicants for leadership positions . . . [and provide] a more exciting approach to administrator preparation—where theory and practice become integrated" (Norris, Hooker, Weise, & Baitland, 1996, p. 10), "build leadership skills [and make] the transition into an administrative position easier" (Barnett et al., 2000, p. 270), and "promote the development of community

. . . and personalize an otherwise anonymous set of experiences for students" (Murphy, 1993, p. 239).

Despite the tendency for cohort members to form close bonds and become a cohesive group, the power of learning communities in the workplace will not be fully realized if learning transfer does not occur. Demonstrating the features of a learning community in a graduate cohort is not enough to ensure that educational leadership programs will develop transformational leaders capable of creating and maintaining similar environments in their schools. We maintain that cohort structures continue to hold great promise for developing transformational leaders (Norris, Barnett, Basom, & Yerkes, 1996); however, the challenge of graduate educational leadership preparation programs lies in the capability of these programs to help aspiring leaders transfer what they learn about learning communities into their school settings. Only when this transfer occurs, will the ultimate legacy of leadership preparation be achieved: the creation of schools as vibrant learning communities, led by confident, competent, and caring transformational leaders.

CONCLUSION

We have argued throughout this book that: (1) learning communities can be created and maintained, (2) transformational leaders are the catalysts for developing and nurturing learning communities, and (3) transformational school leaders can be prepared to establish these communities in their organizations. Nevertheless, the complexity of learning communities does not warrant a formula or step-by-step process that school leaders can employ to ensure that their school settings are places where a sense of collective identity, belongingness, security, and empowerment become part of the culture. We believe that providing a prescriptive action plan for educators, composed of a foolproof set of practices, procedures, and policies, would be a great mistake and disservice to school leaders. Therefore, we have attempted to raise greater awareness of the forces and effects of learning communities by focusing on the conceptual foundations of communities, accounts of our own experiences with learning communities in our leadership development programs, and the types of curricular and instructional practices program developers might consider when attempting to prepare transformational leaders.

Despite the growing interest in and awareness of what learning communities consist of and how leaders can influence their existence, many questions and issues still remain to be answered. Much of the work on learning communities is conceptual and descriptive; empirical studies of the formation and maintenance of learning communities are sparse. Outlined below are a number of areas worth pursuing to further enhance our understanding of the power and fragility of learning communities. Many of these ideas emerge from our earlier work with learning cohorts (Barnett et al., 2000; Barnett & Muth, 2000), where we suggested that future investigations could be shaped by the seminal work on change, particularly organizational factors affecting innovations, the qualities of the change initiative, and how individuals respond to new ideas and practices (e.g., Berman & McLaughlin, 1976; Hall & Hord, 1987; Rogers, 1983).

In particular, we envision the following areas and types of questions as shaping future investigations of learning communities:

> *Internal factors affecting learning communities.* What critical events within the school support or impede the development of a learning community? How do new members of a school setting become acculturated to a learning community? What aspects of the current organizational culture are compatible and incompatible with a learning community? In what ways do the departure and arrival of teachers and leaders affect a learning community?
>
> *External factors affecting learning communities.* What external policies and practices support or erode a learning community? How can a learning community survive in schools during an era of increased organizational competition and accountability? What social, political, and economic trends influence a school's learning community?
>
> *Qualities of a learning community.* How do members of the school organization define a learning community? How does a school's learning community develop over time? What elements of a learning community are observable, elusive, or hidden?
>
> *Impact of learning communities.* What concerns and difficulties do members of a learning community experience? What previous experiences enhance or inhibit an individual's ability to become part of a learning community? How are students, parents, and community members affected when the adults in a school organization have created a learning community?

We view these types of questions as pertinent not only for scholars and researchers, but also for educational practitioners in school settings, school districts, and leadership preparation programs. If our school systems are to overcome such problems as student apathy, teacher and parent disenfranchisement, isolation, and a loss of identity, then discovering ways in which learning communities work is of utmost importance to individuals who work in schools, who prepare professionals for schools, and who seek to investigate how schools can become more effective. Whether the learning community is a group of university researchers who have designed a sophisticated, longitudinal research study or several teachers who are doing action research in their classrooms, understanding what contributes to learning communities and how they affect individuals in school organizations has a promising future for school reform.

Epilogue: The Impact of Our Work, Individually and Collectively

THE GROWTH of the individual as a leader and the development of community are the themes of this book. Throughout, we have examined how these themes are interconnected and how they affect leadership and the preparation of leaders.

University faculty well understand that the development of individuals and groups can be compared to a journey. Few can fail to appreciate the changes in an adult who enters his or her first graduate class in leadership and that same learner, 2 or 3 years later, who has completed a program of study as part of a cohort that has become a learning community.

The beginning student may be timid or self-assured, may or may not have a friend in the group, may have some understanding of leadership, and may be there for a variety of reasons not really known yet. Some enter leadership study confident that they understand much about leadership, and as time goes by come to see that they knew little (Coleman & Yerkes, 1991). Others may have some leadership experience but be unfamiliar with the idiosyncracies of leading educational enterprises. Above all, the student is essentially alone, beginning a journey not taken before.

Through a series of processes and experiences, in which the learners are exposed to themselves and their values, others and their values, content knowledge, skills, problem solving and problem finding, problem-based learning activities and cases, journals, platforms and portfolios, and reflection and research, students travel the path we have described. Students come to understand their own values and reasons for pursuing the course of study. They come to understand their community and how to provide leadership for others in the community. Through interaction with others in the group, they come to understand and clarify their purpose—their own and that of their community. Key to their learning is the direction of facilitative instructors.

The journey of learning takes the cohort through five successive, ascending stages:

- Support, where a comfortable and helpful climate assists them
- Security where they begin to feel confident in themselves and one another
- Friendship, where they join with others by their own choice
- Acquisition of knowledge, where the learning becomes meaningful and they practice the skills they will need as leaders
- Definition and preliminary realization of each member's personal dream

All the while, these adults are moving from independence to interdependence and coming to understand and use the knowledge and practice the skills that will be necessary as they move into a larger learning community as leaders. And all the while, the individuals and the group are learning and growing, simultaneously.

While not every adult learner may reach the highest level of leadership artistry, the effective instructor will attempt throughout the program to assist learners to move, in a systematic way, through the stages of the journey. We are reminded that "cohorts should be deliberately designed to facilitate the development of fully functioning groups and individuals capable of building learning communities and transferring the knowledge of that process to future school settings" (Norris, Barnett, Basom, & Yerkes, 1996, p. 161). Those who lead the nation's schools should be afforded no less than our best efforts to encourage reaching the personal dream. Having experienced these stages and consciously reflected upon the experiences, future leaders learn to work with the learning community entrusted to their care.

While we believed we were studying the cohort—known to some as no more than a convenient device for scheduling students—we realized our work was becoming far more than that. It was clear that there had to be some ways to help graduate students transfer their own learning and experiences to the worlds in which they would work—the administrative offices and hallways and classrooms of schools. We learned that we were studying leadership, learning, teaching, and community.

We are individuals, distinctly different from each other. Three of us come to higher education from K–12 public school backgrounds, having served as administrators in a variety of programs. The other has a distinguished career as a researcher and leadership developer for school administrators. We sometimes talk about how our experience outside the academy has served us in understanding the world of school leadership and creating classes and programs that will prepare people well for the roles they will assume. Without giving away secrets, one might say some of us are more creative than others, some more skilled in organizing our work and plans. Some have broad understanding and experience in curriculum, some in leadership, some in professional development and adult learning, some in research and writing. All are vitally interested in the future of education and in preparing knowledgeable and skilled leaders.

This book continues our efforts to further the development of all—individuals and groups—and we hope it encourages discussion among faculty in departments of leadership and administration. Given the nature of higher education, this will be a long journey. On the other hand, given the changes occurring in higher education with the advances of technology, there could be little time to spend in discussing it to death. We press forward.

OUR REFLECTIONS

We each have grown, and as a group we have grown as well. Each member has contributed reflections about the journey and, typical of our differences, each chose a different method for reporting! We needed a roadmap for this effort as well as for the entire 10 years of work, but, given the nature of the group, it probably would not have made any difference. In an effort to share our experiences in a way that makes sense, we have extrapolated comments from our own reflective journals and remembrances and organized those remarks around the five steps of the cohort model. We believe these remarks provide a means for understanding the reciprocal benefits of learning communities to the individual and to the group, described in Chapter 1. They may serve to inspire faculties or individuals to consider working in community. What a pleasure it is for us to look back and see where our journey has taken us.

Support

The mutual support and solidarity found in true groups (Johnson & Johnson, 1987) was the basis upon which we formed our working relationship. We gradually felt comfortable with each other and realized that we were not in this endeavor alone. Individually, we reflected on "support" as follows:

> Realizing that few people in higher education seemed to be interested in providing support for colleagues, I found within the Dan-

forth group, at some level in the larger group of 25 universities, and later within our small research group, a sense of support not experienced elsewhere in the academy. In fact, I left higher education for a year because the isolation and independence of faculty work behaviors did not suit my style of working. Upon forming our cohort of four, just after this year of personal reflection about career and future, I found others who cared as I did about students and teaching and collaborative work and who wanted to talk about such things.

I love working in groups, and I saw an opportunity for me to learn and grow from great people in our field.

Support comes at different levels. When I joined this group, I was at a midpoint in my career. There were many things that I had done professionally in public education, but my work in higher education was still relatively new. Diane was such a support in those early days! We could commiserate together in terms of our shared experiences: assessment centers, district-level administration, work with teachers in professional development.

Diane was a tremendous support to our group in many ways. She has supported us literally! It was her talent for organization and grant writing that enabled us to secure the funds for operating.

It is uncanny how he [Bruce] can *always* find the avenues to support you—an e-mail, a call, a spoken word of confidence—he seems to always be there! Bruce has been a real professional support to me. He has actually given me the courage to write!

Bruce has been our professional presenter! He has such grace and dignity. He has helped us through the anxiety of presentation in a supportive way.

Peg is our heart and soul! She is able to intuitively sense the heartbeat of the group and radiate that sense of "care" that is necessary during moments of disappointment, tension, and even joy! She epitomizes for me the "servant leader."

Security

As we came to know each other better, trust was built. Our confidence in ourselves and in each other grew. We felt safe admitting what we did not know, in asking others for help, and in having our work critiqued by our colleagues:

> As a nontenured faculty member in the early days, I wondered: Did I know how to do this work? In spite of many years in the field and working with hundreds of school administrators, I lacked confidence in the kind of writing expected of faculty, in research, in presentations at refereed conference sessions.

> To Diane I owe a debt of gratitude that I don't *have to worry!* We will get there! Her facility with detail, time, and structure has provided us all a comfortable base from which to diverge and get off track.

> Peg has taken charge of everything mechanical or technical that seems to create endless "fear" for me: computers, conference calls, budgets, and conference arrangements. What a relief!

Friendship

Just as our graduate students form friendships that last for a long time, we have as well. We became more than a group of faculty working on a project: We valued each other, respected our differences, celebrated individual and collective successes, and genuinely liked each other. For us, friendship was expressed in the following ways:

> Over the years, our friendship has grown. This has been extremely important to me. While we are very different from each other and lived hundreds of miles apart, we had something in common which drew us together. We had goals and plans and in order to meet them, technology notwithstanding, we had to get together. We found ways to stretch our limited grant funding so that we could meet together, at conferences, in the summers in Colorado, even once in Las Vegas. When the funding ran out, we would submit conference proposals and articles so that we would *have* to write and present together. We came to know each other's families, shared events in our lives, followed up on children and aging parents, coming to care for the others in a deep way. And we still talk about working together some day, in some place.

> Another benefit of our working relationship has been to get to know more about one another at a personal level. Involving our

spouses in some of our sessions has been delightful. Whether it's Myron "cooking up" another meal, Don spending an evening with us at Cirque de Soleil, Cynthia recounting a family reunion, or Ann watching a video with us on a rainy night, we came to know each other as members of our families rather than just as college professors. I've developed friendships I rarely establish when working with other colleagues, which I will cherish forever.

Working with my cohort has been a lifesaver. I learned, did research, published, and became known in the world of higher education and in educational leadership through my work with cohort members. We complement each other, we lived through the trials and tribulations of being cohort members, and we developed group goals. At the same time, our individual goals needed to be met. Actually, there were times that Bruce would say, "You need to go first; you need this for your tenure," and in the end we always worked under all four names; the work we produced was far more than single authorship might have been.

Our working styles are different. Cynthia is the dreamer, the visionary, the philosopher, and the theoretical "grounder" for the group. I believe that any new project, new direction, new idea beyond our present thinking was brought to the group through brainstorming and discussions with Cynthia.

Diane is the organizer, the person who knows how to move us from Cynthia's thinking to actually getting it done. She asks all the right questions to move us, to redirect us, to help us get it done.

Bruce is the clarifier. He helps us take visionary ideas and put them into understandable thinking. He questions a lot and massages our thoughts to make them "real." He is the cheerleader of the group. He helps us continue, helps keeps us on the right track and can, better than any of us, make our writing succinct, clear, and readable. His calm, his kindness, and his caring over time have been a real source of strength to us all.

Peg asks clarifying questions. She is good at taking others' thinking and developing it to the next levels. She thinks out loud and brainstorms well. She doesn't get hung up with ego and don't care who gets credit as long as we get things done.

Cynthia doesn't always like bringing her ideas to the whole group. Diane plays the intermediary; Bruce asks tough questions about lofty ideas; Peg can be the peacekeeper in difficult times. All in all we tend to make a good group. We complement strengths, and we balance weaknesses.

The entire group has taught me so much about friendship. The group has been patient with me and with my independent inclinations, and I have learned to really appreciate them as friends and to value our work together. Through my time with this group, I have learned a valuable lesson—no one is complete within themselves! It takes the gifts that all bring to the table to truly complete us as individuals.

Knowledge Acquisition

In settings where people are comfortable and secure and where they enjoy working with their colleagues, group members begin to feel empowered and learning occurs. Our students are taught the importance of learning from each other, as well as the instructor, from reading, discussing, questioning, reflecting, writing, practicing, and receiving feedback from those they trust. Adults learn in such settings, and we did as well:

Cynthia, who knows more about leadership than I can even imagine, who has read and written more than I ever will, who has taught doctoral students all over the country, constantly refining her thinking, is my intellectual mentor.

Nearly every day I learn from Peg and, I hope, improve my own work as a result.

Clearly, many of the readings, assignments, and activities we shared during our sessions have found their way into my teaching.

I've learned as much (if not more) about instructional delivery and curriculum content from our association as I have about cohorts.

It's . . . professionally rewarding to have others in our field comment on our work and be viewed as experts on the subject.

My students have enjoyed the information that I bring back from my meetings with the group. I know what the students are going through with their cohort members because I have experienced it, too.

I cannot begin to express the excitement in learning that this group experience has given to me. Our endless conversations, theorizing, risk-taking, reading, and challenges to each other have made knowledge truly come alive for me. Through our collaborative study, I have been introduced to ideas that I would not have discovered alone. It has been exciting to toss out ideas, watch them come together into patterns, and build from them concepts, presentations, papers, and improved preparation programs! The feelings of stimulation, fulfillment, and confidence have been wonderful to experience. We have all gained a true sense of belonging and pride: This is our group, and together we can accomplish important things!

Personal Dream

While the group can and does enhance one's personal dream, the final step in the model is unique to every individual. Built upon one's own values and desires, it is both professional and personal. It provides the view of oneself in the world (Levinson, 1986) and guides the individual's life and work. Not everyone achieves this level; we believe we, and many of our graduate students, are on the way, as our reflections reveal:

> As a group, our personal dream took shape as the journey progressed. I am pleased that many people quote our work and call us for information. We wanted to make an impact on leadership preparation, and in some ways we have. My hope is that this book will positively influence the work of those who prepare leaders.

> As an individual, my dream—for many years—has been to be a good mentor and teacher to the next generations of school leaders and to write a book about that work. I believe that both are happening; it is reinforcing and rewarding.

> My rewards from working with the group are both professional and personal. Through our research and discussion we've been able to contribute to our understanding of cohorts and how they impact faculty and student development.

My goals have changed but I now am so much more confident in my skills as a professor. I know I can make a difference with students. They are becoming the principals I wanted them to become. I am becoming the person I wanted to be. You [my three colleagues] have been and continue to be the mentors I hope I am to students in this profession.

I have experienced the beauty of leadership and empowerment. I have felt these qualities emerge within myself, and I have watched them emerge within each member of this group. It is a powerful experience to live in community. It empowers, it challenges potential, and it touches the soul. It is uncanny that as I write these words I am in a plane flying over familiar territory. As I gaze out my window, I see in the distance the mountains of Colorado where we worked together. Through the mountain haze I can almost see the images of days past: a mountain retreat . . . a fireplace blazing . . . collections of books and papers scattered across the floor . . . friends gathered for conversation and fun. I remember the food and wine that warmed our hearts . . . the thoughts and friendships that warmed our souls. It has been an unforgettable journey!

THIS CHAPTER OF OUR HISTORY TOGETHER CLOSES

In conclusion, we leave you with the following statement from our reflections:

> The experiences we've shared will live on with each of us. We all have real-life stories to tell about collaboration in higher education. Each time we tell others about what we experienced, we keep the memory of our association alive. Experts on culture remind us that one of the best ways to develop and maintain a shared culture is through storytelling of significant events and the heroes and heroines who shaped these events. So, each time we share "our story" with others, we acknowledge our culture and point out that true collaboration in higher education in not a myth. This is quite a legacy.

In an earlier writing (Norris, Barnett, Basom, & Yerkes, 1996), we described the cohort as a vehicle for building transformational leadership skills in students. It appears we were describing our transformation as well:

Individuals are intricately interwoven into groups and groups become reflections of individuals. Individuals are supported, affirmed, and inspired in groups; they are transformed. In turn, individuals transform groups through their collective efforts and commitment to a meaningful purpose. Groups empower individuals; individuals empower groups. It is a reciprocal process known as community. (p. 145)

References

Achilles, C. M. (1994). Searching for the golden fleece: The epic struggle continues. *Educational Administration Quarterly, 30*(1), 6–26.

Alderfer, C. (1972). *Existence, relatedness, and growth: Human needs in organizational settings.* New York: Free Press.

Apple, M. W., & Beane, J. A. (1995). *Democratic schools.* Alexandria, VA: Association for Supervision and Curriculum Development.

Argyris, C. (1957). The individual and the organization: Some problems of mutual adjustment. *Administrative Science Quarterly, 2,* 1–24.

Argyris, C., & Schön, D. A. (1974). *Theory in practice: Increasing professional effectiveness.* San Francisco: Jossey-Bass.

Ashby, D. E. (2000, March). *The standards issue in preparing school leaders: Moving toward higher quality preparation and assessment.* Paper presented at the conference of the American Association of School Administrators, San Francisco.

Baitland, B. (1992). *An evaluation of an experiential school principal preparation program at the University of Houston.* University of Houston, Houston.

Ballering, L. (1997). *Practicing administrators' attitudes toward the ethic of care.* Doctoral dissertation, University of Houston, Houston.

Barnard, C. I. (1968a). *Functions of the executive* (2nd ed.). Cambridge, MA: Harvard University Press.

Barnard, C. I. (1968b). Mind in everyday affairs (Cyrus Fogg Bracket Lecture, presented to the engineering faculty and students of Princeton University, March 10, 1936). In C. I. Barnard, *Functions of the executive* (2nd ed., pp. 302–322). Cambridge, MA: Harvard University Press.

Barnett, B. (1991). The educational platform: Articulating moral dilemmas and choices for future educational leaders. In B. Barnett, F. McQuarrie, & C. Norris (Eds.), *The moral dimensions of leadership: A focus on human decency* (pp. 129–153). Memphis, TN: Memphis State University, National Network for Innovative Principal Preparation.

Barnett, B. (1992). Using alternative assessment measures in educational leadership preparation programs: Educational platforms and portfolios. *Journal of Personnel Evaluation in Education, 6,* 141–151.

Barnett, B., Basom, M., Yerkes, D., & Norris, C. (2000). Cohorts in educational leadership programs: Benefits, difficulties and the potential for developing school leaders. *Educational Administration Quarterly, 36*(2), 255–282.

Barnett, B. G., Hall, G. E., Berg, J. B., & Camarena, M. M. (1999). A typology of partnerships for promoting innovation. *Journal of School Leadership, 6*(9), 484–510.

Barnett, B., & Muse, I. D. (1993). Cohort groups in educational administration: Promises and challenges. *Journal of School Leadership, 3*(4), 400–415.

Barnett, B., & Muth, R. (2000, November). *Making the case for professional preparation: Using research for program improvement and political support.* Paper presented at the annual convention of the University Council for Educational Administration, Albuquerque, NM, November.

Barnett, B., & O'Mahony, G. (n.d.). *Reflection as the foundation for professional development: Implications for individual and team learning.* Unpublished manuscript.

Basom, M. R., Yerkes, D. M., Norris, C., & Barnett, B. (1996). Using cohorts as a means for developing transformational leaders. *Journal of School Leadership, 6*(1), 99–112.

Bass, B. (1985). *Leadership and performance beyond expectations.* New York: Free Press.

Beach, K. (1999). Consequential transitions: A sociocultural expedition beyond transfer in education. *Review of research in education, 24,* 101–139.

Beck, L. (1994). *Reclaiming educational administration as a caring profession.* New York: Teachers College Press.

Beck, L., & Murphy, J. (1997). *Ethics in educational leadership programs: Emerging models.* Columbia, MO: University Council of Educational Administration.

Berman, P., & McLaughlin, M. W. (1976). Implementation of educational innovations. *Educational Forum, 40,* 345–370.

Blankstein, A., & Sandoval, G. (1998). In gangs we trust: A close up of the new induction. *Reaching Today's Youth: The Community Circle of Caring Journal, 3*(1), 24–27.

Blumberg, A. (1989). *Administration as craft.* New York: Longmans.

Bolman, L., & Deal, T. (1991). *Reframing organizations: Artistry, choice and leadership.* San Francisco: Jossey–Bass.

Bransford, J. D., & Schwartz, D. L. (1999). Rethinking transfer: A simple proposal with multiple implications. *Review of research in education, 24,* 61–100. Washington, DC:

Brent, B. O. (1998). Should graduate training in educational administration be required for principal certification? Existing evidence suggests the answer is no. *Teaching in Educational Administration Newsletter, 5*(2), 1, 3–8.

Brent, B. O., & Haller, E. J. (1998). Who really benefits from graduate training in educational administration? *The AASA Professor, 21*(1), 1–7.

Bridges, E. M. (1992). *Problem based learning for administrators.* Eugene, OR: ERIC Clearinghouse on Educational Management.

Bridges, E. M., & Hallinger, P. (1997). Using problem-based learning to prepare educational leaders. *Peabody Journal of Education, 72* (2), 131–146.

Brilhart, J. K., & Galanes, G. (1992). *Effective group discussion.* Dubuque, IA: WCB.

Brooks, M. G., & Grennon, J. (1999). The courage to be constructivist. *Educational Leadership, 57*(3), 18–24.

Broudy, H. S. (1977). Types of knowledge and purposes of education. In R. C.

Anderson, R. J. Spiro, & W. E. Montague (Eds.), *Schooling and the acquisition of knowledge* (pp. 1–17). Hillsdale, NJ: Erlbaum.

Brubaker, D. (1994). *Creative curriculum leadership*. Thousand Oaks, CA: Corwin Press.

Buckingham, M., & Coffman, C. (1999). *First, break all the rules*. New York: Simon & Schuster.

Burns, J. M. (1978). *Leadership*. New York: Harper & Row.

Caffarella, R. S. (in press). *Planning programs for adult learners: A practical guide for educators, trainers and staff developers* (2nd ed.). San Francisco: Jossey-Bass.

Cartwright, D. (1968). The nature of group cohesiveness. In D. Cartwright & A. Zander, *Group dynamic research and theory* (pp. 91–109). New York: Harper & Row.

Cohen, D. (1976). Loss as a theme in social policy. *Harvard Educational Review, 46,* 553–571.

Coleman, D. (2000). Reliability and validity of ISLLC: Standards. *The AASA Professor, 23*(2), 7–8.

Coleman, D., & Yerkes, D. (1991). After one course: A study of changes in perceived competence held by teachers beginning a graduate program in educational administration. *Journal of California Association of Professors of Educational Administration, 3*(1), 3–22.

Cooper, B., & Boyd, W. (1987). The evolution of training for school administrators. In J. Murphy & P. Hallinger (Eds.), *Approaches to administrative training in education* (pp. 3–27). Albany: State University of New York Press.

Council of Chief State School Officers. (1996). *Interstate school leaders licensure consortium: Standards for school leaders*. Washington, DC: Author.

Covey, S. R. (1989). *Seven habits of highly effective people*. New York: Simon & Schuster.

Covrig, D. M. (1999). *Conflicting commitments in the life of professionals: Toward a new communitarian professional ethic*. Draft of presentation at the annual meeting of the American Educational Research Association, Montreal.

Cunningham, W. (1983). Teacher burnout: Solutions for the 1980's. *The Urban Review, 15*(1), 37–51.

Daudelin, M. W. (1996, Winter). Learning from experience through reflection. *Organizational Dynamics*, Winter, *28*(2), 36–48.

Deal, T. E., & Peterson, K. D. (1999). *Shaping school culture: The heart of leadership*. San Francisco: Jossey-Bass.

Detterman, D. K. (1993). The case for the prosecution: Transfer as an epiphenomenon. In D. K. Detterman & R. J. Sternberg (Eds.), *Transfer on trial: Intelligence, cognition, and instruction* (pp. 1–24). Norwood, NJ: Ablex.

Detterman, D. K., & Sternberg, R. J. (Eds.). (1993). *Transfer on trial: Intelligence, cognition, and instruction*. Norwood, NJ: Ablex.

Dewey, J. (1938). *Experience and education*. New York: Macmillan.

Driekurs, R., Grunwald, B. B., & Peppers, F. C. (1982). *Maintaining sanity in the classroom*. New York: Harper & Row.

Drucker, P. F. (1999). *Management challenges for the 21st century*. New York: Harper Business.

Dworkin, A. G. (1987). *Teacher burnout in the public schools*. Albany: State University of New York Press.

Erlandson, D. A., Skrla, L., Westbrook, D., Hornback, S., & Mindiz-Melton, A. (1999). Reshaping urban education: A school–community–university collaborative initiative. *Journal of School Leadership, 6*(9), 552–573.

Farber, B. A. (1984). Teacher burnout: Assumptions, myths, and issues. *Teachers College Record, 86*(2), 321–338.

Fleisher, M. (1985, March). *Routinization of a psychology program: Passages and cycles*. Paper presented at the annual meeting of the Eastern Psychological Association, Boston.

Forsyth, D. R. (1990). *Group dynamics*. Pacific Grove, CA: Brooks/Cole.

Foster, W. (1986). Toward a critical practice of leadership. In J. Smyth (Ed.), *Critical perspectives on educational leadership* (pp. 39–62). Philadelphia: Falmer Press.

Freed, C. (1999). Round pegs in square holes: The many faces of systemic failure. *Journal for a Just and Caring Education, 5* (4), 462–475.

Fullan, M. (1993). *Change forces: Probing the depths of educational reform*. New York: Falmer Press.

Fusarelli, L. D., & Smith, L. (1999). Improving urban schools via leadership: Preparing administrators for the new millennium. *Journal of School Leadership, 6*(9), 534–551.

Gardner, H. (1995). *Leading minds: An anatomy of leadership*. New York: Basic Books.

Gardner, J. W. (1989, Fall). Building community. *Kettering Review*, pp. 73–81.

Gilligan, C. (1982). *In a different voice: Psychological theory and women's development*. Cambridge, MA: Harvard University Press.

Glaser, B. (1965). The constant comparative method of qualitative analysis. *Social Problems, 12*, 436–445.

Goldman, P., & Kempner, K. (1988). *The administrator's view of professional training*. (ERIC Document Reproduction Service No. ED 325 979)

Goodlad, J. (1984). *A place called school*. New York: McGraw-Hill.

Goodlad, J. (1994). *Educational renewal: Better teachers, better schools*. San Francisco: Jossey-Bass.

Greenleaf, R. (1977). *Servant leadership: A journey into the nature of legitimate power and greatness*. New York: Paulist Press.

Griffiths, D. E. (1977). Preparation programs for administrators. In L. L. Cunningham, W. G. Hack, & R. O. Nystrand (Eds.), *Educational administration: The developing decades* (pp. 401–437). Berkeley: McCutchan.

Griffiths, D., Stout, R., & Forsyth, P. (1988). The preparation of educational administrators. In D. Griffiths, R. Stout, & P. Forsyth (Eds.), *Leaders for America's schools* (pp. 284–304). Berkeley: McCutchan.

Guskey, T. R., & Sparks, D. (1991, March). *Complexities in evaluating the effects of staff development programs*. Paper presented at the annual meeting of the American Educational Research Association, Chicago.

Hall, B. (1976). *The development of consciousness: A confluent theory of values*. New York: Paulist Press.

Hall, B., Kalven, J., Rosen, L., & Taylor, B. (1991). *Developing human values*. Fond Du Lac, WI: International Values Institute of Marian College.

Hall, B., & Thompson, H. (1980). *Leadership through values*. New York: Paulist Press.

Hall, G. E., & Hord, S. M. (1987). *Change in schools: Facilitating the process*. Albany: State University of New York Press.

Haller, E. J., Brent, B., & McNamara, J. F. (1997). Does graduate training in educational administration improve America's schools? Another look at some national data. *Phi Delta Kappan, 79*, 222–227.

Hannay, L. M. (1994). Strategies for facilitating reflective practice: The role of staff developers. *Journal of Staff Development, 15*(3), 22–26.

Hare, A. (1952). Interaction and consensus in different size groups. *American Sociological Review, 17*, 261–267.

Henderson, J. G., & Hawthorne, R. D. (1995). *Transformative curriculum leadership*. Englewood Cliffs, NJ: Merrill.

Herbert, F., & Reynolds, K. (n.d.). *Cohort groups and intensive schedules: Does familiarity breed learning?* Unpublished manuscript.

Hersey, P., & Blanchard, K. (1982). Leadership style: Attitudes and behaviors. *Training and Development, 36*, 50–52.

Herzberg, F. (1968). One more time: How do you motivate employees? *Harvard Business Review, 46*(4), 53–62.

Hill, M. (n.d.). Leadership preparation: Self reflection and self assessment. *Design for Leadership* (Bulletin of the National Policy Board for Educational Administration).

Hill, M. (1992). *Graduate cohorts: Perceptions of benefits and catalysts to cohesiveness of 19 heads are better than one*. Unpublished manuscript.

Hill, M. (1995). Educational leadership cohort models: Changing the talk to change the walk. *Planning and Changing, 26*(3/4), 179–189.

Hodgkinson, C. (1983). *The philosophy of leadership*. Oxford: Blackwell.

Hole, S., & McEntee, G. H. (1999). Reflection is at the heart of practice. *Educational Leadership, 56*(8), 34–37.

Holland, P., & Weise, K. (1999). Helping novice teachers. In L. Hughes (Ed.), *Principal as leader* (2nd ed.; pp. 182–212). Columbus, OH: Merrill.

Hunter, M. (1971). *Teach for transfer*. El Segundo, CA: TIP Publications.

Johnson, D. W., & Johnson, R. T. (1987). *Joining together: Group theory and group skills*. Englewood Cliffs, NJ: Prentice Hall.

Johnson, D. W., & Johnson, R. T. (1996). *Meaningful and manageable assessment through cooperative learning*. Edina, MN: Interaction Book Company.

Johnson, D. W., Johnson, R. T., & Smith, K. A. (1991). *Active learning: Cooperation in the college classroom*. Edina, MN: Interaction Book Company.

Kasten, K. (1992, October). *Students' perceptions of the cohort model of instructional delivery*. Paper presented at the annual convention of the University Council of Educational Administration, Minneapolis.

Kerrins, J. A., & Cushing, K. S. (1997, March). *Extending the learning: Using rubrics to foster reflection*. Paper presented at the annual meeting of the American Educational Research Association, Chicago.

King, P., & Kitchener, K. (1994). *Developing reflective judgment*. San Francisco: Jossey–Bass.

Knowles, M. (1980). *The modern practice of adult education: From pedagogy to andragogy* (2nd ed.). New York: Cambridge Books.

Knowles, M. (1985). *Andragogy in action.* San Francisco: Jossey-Bass.

Kohlberg, L. (1981). *The philosophy of moral development: Moral stages and the idea of justice.* Cambridge: Harper & Row.

Kolb, D. (1984). *Experiential learning.* Englewood Cliffs, NJ: Prentice Hall.

Kottkamp, R. (1982). The administrative platform in administrative preparation. *Planning and Changing, 13,* 82–92.

Kottkamp, R. (1990). Facilitating reflection. *Education and Urban Society, 22*(2), 182–203.

Kouzes, J. M., & Posner, B. Z. (1987). *The leadership challenge: How to get extraordinary things done in organizations.* San Francisco: Jossey-Bass.

Kouzes, J. M., & Posner, B. Z. (1990). *Leadership practices inventory.* San Diego: Pfeiffer.

Kouzes, J., & Posner, B. (1993). *Credibility.* San Francisco: Jossey-Bass.

Krathwohl, D. (1964). *Taxonomy of educational objectives: The classification of educational goals: Handbook II. Affective domain.* New York: David McKay.

Kultgen, J. (1988). *Ethics and professionalism.* Philadelphia: University of Pennsylvania Press.

Lebsack, J. (1993). *A formative evaluation of a university departmental restructuring effort.* Unpublished doctoral dissertation, University of Houston, Houston.

Lee, A. Y. (1998). Transfer as a measure of intellectual functioning. In S. Soraci & W. J. McIlvane (Eds.), *Perspectives on fundamental processes in intellectual functioning: A survey of research approaches* (Vol. 1, pp. 351–366). Stamford, CT: Ablex.

Lee, A. Y., & Pennington, N. (1993). Learning computer programming: A route to general reasoning skills? In C. R. Cook, J. C. Scholtz, & J. C. Spohrer (Eds.), *Empirical studies of programmers: Fifth workshop* (pp. 113–136). Norwood, NJ: Ablex.

Leithwood, K., Jantzi, D., & Coffin, G. (1995). *Preparing school leaders: What works.* Toronto: Ontario Institute for Studies in Education.

Levine, S. (1989). *Promoting adult growth in schools.* Boston: Allyn & Bacon.

Levinson, D. (1986). A conception of adult development. *American Psychologist, 41*(1), 7.

Lightfoot, S. (1983). *The good high school: Portraits of character and culture.* New York: Basic Books.

Little, J. (1993). Teachers' professional development in a climate of educational reform. *Educational Evaluation and Policy Analysis, 15*(2), 129–151.

Little, J. W., & McLaughlin, M. W. (Eds.). (1993). *Teachers' work: Individuals, colleagues, and contexts.* New York: Teachers College Press.

Loeser, L. (1957). Some aspects of group dynamics. *International Journal of Group Psycho Therapy, 7*(1) 5–19.

Loevinger, J. (1976). *Ego development: Conceptions and theories.* San Francisco: Jossey-Bass.

Marini, A., & Genereux, R. (1995). The challenge of teaching for transfer. In A. McKeough, J. Lupart, & A. Marini (Eds.), *Teaching for transfer: Fostering generalization in learning* (pp. 1–19). Mahwah, NJ: Erlbaum.

Marshall, C., & Kasten, K. (1994). *The administrative career: A casebook on entry, equity, and endurance.* Thousand Oaks, CA: Corwin Press.

Maslach, C. (1982). *Burnout: The cost of caring.* Englewood Cliffs, NJ: Prentice Hall.

Maslow, A. (1976). Toward a psychology of being. In A. Rothenburg & C. Housman (Eds.), *The creativity question* (pp. 296–305). Durham, NC: Duke University Press.

May, L. (1996). *The socially responsive self: Social theory and professional ethics.* Chicago: University of Chicago Press.

McBrien, J. L., & Brandt, R. S. (1997). *The language of learning: A guide to education terms.* Alexandria, VA: Association for Supervision and Curriculum Development.

McClellan, D. (1976). Power is the great motivation. *Harvard Business Review, 54*(2), 100.

McGrath, J., & Altman, I. (1966). *Small group research.* New York: Holt, Rinehart & Winston.

McNeil, J. (1985). *Curriculum: A comprehensive introduction* (3rd ed.). Boston: Little, Brown.

Melaville, A. I., Blank, J., & Asayesh, G. (1993). *Together we can: A guide for crafting a profamily system of education and human services.* Washington, DC: U.S. Department of Education and U.S. Department of Health and Human Services.

Merriam, S. B., & Caffarella, R. S. (1991). *Learning in adulthood.* San Francisco: Jossey-Bass.

Miller, R. (1990). *What are schools for?* Brandon, VT: Holistic Education Press.

Milstein, M. M., & Associates. (1993). *Changing the way we prepare educational leaders: The Danforth experience.* Newbury Park, CA: Corwin Press.

Milstein, M. M., & Krueger, J. (1993). Innovative approaches to clinical internships: The University of New Mexico experience. In J. Murphy (Ed.), *Preparing tomorrow's school leaders: Alternative designs* (pp. 19–38). University Park, PA: University Council for Educational Administration.

Mintzberg, H. (1976). Planning on the left side and managing on the right. *Harvard Business Review, 54*(4), 49–58.

Morgan, G. (1986). *Images of organizations.* Newbury Park, CA: Sage.

Murphy, J. F. (1990). Restructuring the technical core of preparation programs in educational administration. *UCEA Review, 31*(3), 4–5, 10–13.

Murphy, J. (1992). *The landscape of leadership preparation: Reframing the education of school administrators.* Newbury Park, CA: Corwin Press.

Murphy, J. (1993). *Preparing tomorrow's school leaders: Alternative designs.* University Park, PA: University Council for Educational Administration.

National Center for Education Statistics. (1998). *Parent involvement in children's education: Efforts by public elementary schools* (Report No. 98–032). Washington, DC: Author.

National Commission for the Principalship. (1990). *Principals for our changing schools: Preparation and certification.* Fairfax, VA: Author.

Noddings, N. (1984). *Caring: A feminine approach to ethics and moral education.* Berkeley: University of California Press.

Norris, C. (1999). Cultivating creative cultures. In L. Hughes (Ed.), *Principal as leader* (2nd ed.; pp. 60–88). Columbus, OH: Merrill.

Norris, C., & Achilles, C. (1987). Intuitive leadership: A new dimension for educational leadership. *Planning and Changing, 19*(2), 108–117.

Norris, C., & Barnett, B. (1994, October). *Cultivating a new leadership paradigm: From cohorts to communities.* Paper presented at the annual meeting of the University Council of Educational Administration, Philadelphia.

Norris, C., Barnett, B., Basom, M., & Yerkes, D. (1996). The cohort: A vehicle for building transformational leadership skills. *Planning and Changing, 27*(3/4), 145–164.

Norris, C., Basom, M., Yerkes, D., & Barnett, B. (1996, October). *The development of platforms in leadership programs: Perspectives and prospects.* Paper presented at annual conference of the University Council for Educational Administration, Louisville, KY. (ERIC Document Reproduction Service No. EA 028 098)

Norris, C., Herrmond, D., & Meisgeier, C. (1996). Developing creative leaders for empowered schools. *National Forum of Educational Administration and Supervision Journal, 14*(1), 14–29.

Norris, C., Hooker, R., Weise, K. & Baitland, B. (1996, October). *A community of learners: University and district collaboration.* Paper presented at the annual conference of the University Council for Educational Administration, Louisville, KY.

Norton, M. S. (1995, October). *The status of student cohorts in educational administration preparation programs.* Paper presented at the annual conference of the University Council for Educational Administration, Salt Lake City, UT.

Ottoson, J. M. (1995). Use of a conceptual framework to explore multiple influences on the application of learning following a continuing education program. *CJSAE/RCEEA, 9*(2), 1–17.

Parsons, T. (1951). *The social system.* New York: Free Press.

Peck, S. (n.d.). [Interview]. *Bottom Line/Personal,* n.p.

Piaget, J. (1970). Piaget's theory. In P. Mussen (Ed.), *Carmichael's manual of child psychology* (3rd ed.; Vol. 1, pp. 703–732). New York: Wiley.

Razik, R., & Swanson, A. (2001). *Fundamental concepts of educational leadership* (2nd ed.). Upper Saddle River, NJ: Prentice Hall.

Requisites of a leader, Available: http://www.requisitesofaleader.com

Rogers, E. M. (1969). *Freedom to learn.* New York: Merrill.

Rogers, E. M. (1983). *Diffusion of innovations.* New York: Free Press.

Schein, E. H. (1992). *Organizational culture and leadership* (2nd ed.). San Francisco: Jossey-Bass.

Schnur, S. I. (1989). The training of educational administrators: Perceptions of building principals. *Dissertation Abstracts International, 50,* 11A.

Schön, D. (1983). *The reflective practitioner: How professionals think and act.* New York: Basic Books.

Schwahn, C. (1998). *Component V: Portfolio based assessment* (personal draft copy from author). Schwahn Leadership Associates, Custer, SD.

Senge, P. M. (1990). *The fifth discipline.* New York: Doubleday.

Sergiovanni, T. (1990). *Value-added leadership: How to get extraordinary performance schools.* San Francisco: Harcourt Brace Jovanovich.

Sergiovanni, T. (1992). *Moral leadership: Getting to the heart of school improvement.* San Francisco: Jossey-Bass.

Sergiovanni, T., & Starratt, R. (1979). *Supervision: Human perspectives*. New York: McGraw-Hill.

Sergiovanni, T., & Starratt, R. (1993). *Supervision: A redefinition* (3rd ed.). New York: McGraw-Hill.

Shaw, M. (1981). *Group dynamics: The psychology of small group behavior*. New York: McGraw Hill.

Short, P. M., & Twale, D. J. (1994). Educational administrators as leaders: Instructional implications. In T. A. Mulkeen, N. H. Cambron-McCabe, & B. J. Anderson (Eds.), *Democratic leadership: The changing context of administrative preparation* (pp. 33–44). Norwood, NJ: Ablex.

Sparks-Langer, G. M., Simmons, J. M., Pasch, M., Colton, A., & Starko, A. (1990). Reflective pedagogical thinking: How can we promote it and measure it? *Journal of Teacher Education, 41*(5), 23–32.

Starratt, R. J. (1995). *Leaders with vision*. Thousand Oaks, CA: Corwin Press.

Starratt, R. J. (1996). *Transforming educational administration, meaning, community and excellence*. New York: McGraw-Hill.

Strain, J. M. (1993). *A comparative study of African-American, Anglo-American, and Hispanic-American dropouts and African-American, Anglo-American, and Hispanic-American graduates in an urban public school system*. Unpublished doctoral dissertation, University of Houston, Houston.

Strike, K., Haller, E., & Soltis, J. (1988). *The ethics of school administration*. New York: Teachers College Press.

Tannenbaum, R., & Schmidt, W. (1958). How to choose a leadership pattern. *Harvard Business Review, 36*, 95–101.

Tracom Corporation. (1981). *Styles awareness training: Improving interpersonal skills with social style*. Denver: Author.

Trubowitz, S. (1986). Stages in the development of school–college collaboration. *Educational Leadership, 43*(5), 18–21.

Trueba, H., Spindler, G., & Spindler, L. (1989). *What do anthropologists have to say about dropouts? The First Centennial Conference on Children at Risk*. Philadelphia: Falmer Press.

Tucker, M. C., & Codding, J. B. (1998). *Standards for our schools: How to set them, measure them and reach them*. San Francisco: Jossey-Bass.

Ubben, G., Hughes, L., & Norris, C. (2001). *The principal*. New York: Allyn & Bacon.

Vince, R. (1998). Behind and beyond Kolb's learning cycle. *Journal of Management Education, 22*(3), 304–319.

Vygotsky, L. S. (1978). *Mind in society: The development of higher psychological processes*. Cambridge, MA: Harvard University Press.

Wasserman, S. (1991). Louis E Raths' theories of empowerment. *Childhood Education*, pp. 235–239.

Weise, K. R. (1992). *A contemporary historical study of the Danforth Principal Preparation Program at the University of Houston*. Unpublished doctoral dissertation, University of Houston, Houston.

Whitaker, K. S., & Barnett, B. G. (1999). A partnership model linking K–12 school districts and leadership preparation programs. *Planning and Changing, 30*, 136–143.

White, E. M. (1990). The damage of innovations set adrift. *American Association for Higher Education Bulletin, 43*(3), 3–5.

Wilson, P. (1993). Pushing the edge. In M. M. Milstein & Associates, *Changing the way we prepare educational leaders: The Danforth experience.* Newbury Park, CA: Corwin Press.

Wingspread Group in Higher Education. (1993). *An American imperative: Higher expectations for higher education.* Racine WI: Johnson Foundation.

Yerkes, D., Norris, C., Basom, P., & Barnett, B. (1994, Spring). Exploring cohorts: Effects on principal preparation and leadership practice. *Connections: Conversations on Issues of Principal Preparation, 2*(3), 1, 5–8.

Zaleznik, A. (1977). Managers and leaders: Are they different? *Harvard Business Review, 55*(3), 67–78.

Zander, A. (1982). *Making groups effective.* San Francisco: Jossey-Bass.

Index

Accountability, 14, 67, 85, 87, 92, 102, 121
Achilles, C. M., 28, 115
Administrators, 11, 49, 66. *See also* Leadership development/leadership development programs; Principals
Adult learning theory, 2, 88-89, 96, 97, 98, 100, 101
Alderfer, C., 12
Altman, I., 14
American Association of School Administrators, 93
Apple, M. W., 93, 99, 103, 108
Argyris, Chris, 44, 83, 84, 86, 106
Ashby, D. E., 95-96, 109
Assessment: authentic, 102, 103, 106; and curriculum, 95, 96, 102, 103, 105, 106-7; feedback about, 105; personality, 50; and principals as developing leaders, 50, 51, 72-73; of professors, 96; self-, 48, 50, 103, 105, 107. *See also type of assessment*
Authoritative leadership, 40, 82, 84
Autocratic leadership, 82

Baitland, B., 3, 125
Ballering, L., 88
Barnard, Chester, 14, 28, 91
Barnett, Bruce G., 2-3, 6, 9, 13, 14, 15, 20, 49, 73, 75, 97, 99, 100, 101, 102, 103, 104, 105, 110, 117, 118, 122, 123, 125, 126, 127, 129-38
Basom, M., 3, 14, 15, 20, 49, 73, 99, 102, 110, 117, 125, 126, 130, 137
Bass, B., 6, 84
Beach, K., 111
Beane, J. A., 93, 99, 103, 108
Beck, L., 36, 37, 78
Benevolent/authority leadership, 82, 84

Berman, P., 115, 121, 127
Blanchard, K., 13
Blankstein, A., 11
Blumberg, A., 106
Bolman, L., 28
Boyd, W., 84, 92
Brandt, R. S., 97
Bransford, J. D., 110, 112, 114, 116, 119
Brent, B. O., 92, 117, 118
Bridges, E. M., 107, 111
Brilhart, J. K., 100
Broad, Eli, 94
Brooks, M. G., 97, 103
Broudy, H. S., 110, 112
Brubaker, D., 13
Buckingham, M., 99
Bureaucratic leadership, 82, 84-85
Burns, J. M., 6, 46, 81, 82

Caffarella, R. S., 97, 100, 101, 103, 111, 113, 114, 115, 121, 122, 123
California State University, Fresno, 2, 15, 50-51, 60. *See also* Williams, Ross
Care, 10, 22, 89, 98; ethic of, 10, 37, 41, 76, 77, 78-79, 86, 89, 98; moral leadership through, 75-78; for others, 76, 77, 78, 79; phases of, 78-79; by professors, 88; of self, 76, 77, 78; of self and others, 76, 78; and transformational leadership, 86, 87, 88; and values, 37, 41, 44
Cartwright, D., 14
Change: and impact of work about leadership development, 129-31; and learning communities, 28, 118, 125, 127, 128; and learning transfer, 112-16; and nature of leadership, 32, 34; and personal dream, 34; and principals as developing leaders,

149

Change (*Continued*)
  68, 71; and school reform as deficit models, 73; and servant leadership, 81; and
  transformational leadership, 87; and values, 32, 34, 39
Charismatic leadership, 82
Cicero, 51
Codding, J. B., 103
Coffman, C., 99
Cohorts: and beliefs/assumptions of learning communities, 10; and curriculum,
  102; and development of learning communities, 1, 118, 119, 120–21; differences
  between workplace and, 120–21; importance of, 126; and individual development, 21; and learning transfer, 116; and
  nature of groups, 14, 15; and principals
  as developing leaders, 50, 51, 65, 67; pur-
  pose/function of, 130; size of, 121;
  stages in, 130; structure of, 126; study of,
  3–4, 15–16, 129–38; and transformational leadership, 88, 137–38. *See also*
  Learning communities; *specific cohort*
Coleman, D., 95, 141
Collaboration: and benefits of leadership
  preparation programs, 118; and curriculum, 101, 102, 105, 108, 109; and empowerment, 13; factors inhibiting, 19; and
  learning communities, 10, 12, 21, 25, 120,
  121, 122; and nature of groups, 15, 19;
  and principals as developing leaders, 74;
  and transformational leadership, 87; and
  values, 43, 45
Commitment, 13, 23, 79, 119; and curriculum, 99–100; and leadership modes, 81,
  82, 83, 84; and nature of leadership, 32,
  33; and principals as developing leaders,
  51, 52, 66; and values, 32, 33, 35, 45, 46
Communal/collaborative growth cycle, 41,
  42, 43, 55, 76, 77, 78, 82
Community: and care, 76, 77; characteristics of, 9; and curriculum, 94; definition
  of, 77; functions of, 77; and impact of
  work about leadership development,
  138; and nature of leadership, 33; and
  principals as developing leaders, 66, 67,
  69, 70; and transformational leadership,
  88; and values, 31–47. *See also* Learning
  communities
Conformist values stage, 38, 39, 41

Connections, 9, 17, 20, 22, 36, 86, 87, 99.
  See also Relationships
Conscientious-conformist values stage, 38–
  39, 41
Content, 7, 12, 40, 91, 92–96, 109, 118
Context, 5, 40, 42, 45, 46, 98, 112, 115–16,
  120
Cooper, B., 84, 92
Cooperative-learning activities, 108. *See
  also* Collaboration
Cooperative-learning groups. *See* Learning
  communities
Council of Chief State School Officers
  (CCSSO), 93, 94
Covey, S. R., 73
Covrig, D. M., 34
Crawford, Bob, 65–71
Credibility, 13, 32–33, 48, 58, 63, 74, 89
Cunningham, W., 11
Curriculum: and challenge to those who
  prepare leaders, 89; constructivist approach to, 2, 96, 97–98, 101, 103; con-
  tent-driven, 7, 92–96; criticisms of, 92–
  93, 94; to foster leadership development,
  91–109; and group development, 96, 98,
  99–100; humanistic, 98, 100; and individual development, 96, 98–99; and instructional methods, 100–108; interdisciplinary approach to, 98; and knowledge, 7;
  and leadership modes, 7, 84; NCATE
  guidelines for, 93; overview about, 7;
  and principals as developing leaders, 73;
  process-driven, 7, 91, 96–100, 109; purposes of, 7, 91; and role of professor,
  100–102; social reconstructionist approach to, 104; standards for, 7, 93–96,
  103, 108, 109; and values, 7, 36
Cushing, K. S., 104

Dahl, Robert, 83
Danforth Foundation, 3–4, 50
Daudelin, M. W., 113, 123
Deal, T., 28, 121
Decision making, 32, 68, 70, 97, 100, 121
Detterman, D. K., 110, 112, 115, 120
Dewey, John, 97, 99
Dialogue, 29, 30, 33, 34, 36, 46, 86, 87, 89
Discourse, 29
Discussions, 13, 33
Disengagement, 11–12, 87

Disposition, 1, 7, 9, 10, 37, 40, 109, 118
Domain 8, 95
Dreams. *See* Personal dream; Visions
Dreikurs, R., 12
Drucker, P. F., 99
Dutot High School (Wyoming): Norman at, 56–60
Dworkin, A. G., 11

Education: aims/purpose of, 49, 53, 67, 69, 71, 73
Educators: role of, 52. *See also type of educator*
Ego development, 38–40
Empowerment: and benefits of leadership preparation programs, 118; and challenge to those who prepare leaders, 88, 90; characteristics of personal, 12; communities as fostering, 9; and curriculum, 98, 104, 109; definition of, 12; and impact of work about leadership development, 137, 138; and individual development, 22, 23; and learning communities, 2, 7, 14, 25, 120; and principals as developing leaders, 62–63, 68; theoretical underpinnings of, 1–13, 88–89; and transfer to workplace, 126; and transformational leadership, 87; and values, 46, 85
Enabling leadership, 82
Erlandson, D. A., 122
Espoused theory, 5, 46, 86, 89, 106; and nature of leadership, 32–33; and principals as developing leaders, 48, 49–50, 51–52, 54, 55, 56–57, 58, 60–62, 63, 65–67, 69, 71–72
Ethics, 36–38, 85–87, 92. *See also* Care: ethic of; Justice: ethnic of
Experiential learning, 7, 33, 37, 89–90, 104, 113. *See also* Knowledge/knowledge acquisition: shared

Facilitators, 3–4, 45, 101, 102, 129
Familial growth cycle, 40, 41, 42, 43, 76, 78, 82
Families. *See* Parents/families
Farber, B. A., 11
Feedback, 15, 48, 50, 65, 72, 99, 105–6
Fieldwork, 2, 50, 60, 65, 104
Fleisher, M., 115

Followers, 40–41, 46, 80–81, 85
Forsyth, D. R., 101
Foster, W., 6, 76, 85–86
Friendship, 4, 21, 22–23, 25, 36, 39, 40, 78, 130, 133–35
Fullan, M., 121
Fusarelli, L. D., 122

Galanes, G., 100
Gardner, H., 32
Gardner, J. W., 12
Gates Foundations, 94
Genereux, R., 112
Getting-acquainted activities, 102, 108
Gilligan, C., 38, 75, 76–77, 78
Glaser, B., 15
Goldman, P., 117
Goodlad, J., 11, 75, 87
Greenleaf, R., 6, 75, 79, 80, 81, 88
Grennon, J., 97, 103
Griffiths, D. E., 84, 101
Group projects, 13, 18, 23, 108. *See also* Collaboration
Groups: and curriculum, 96, 98, 99–100; development of, 9, 16–19, 20, 24–25, 83, 85, 96, 98, 99–100, 129–31; frequency and quality of interaction in, 14; and impact of work about leadership development, 129–31; individual applications versus, 119–20; and leadership modes, 83, 85; and learning communities, 9, 24–25, 119–20, 124; needs of, 14; purpose of, 14–15, size of, 14, 102; sociological and psychological nature of, 14–15, 16–19. *See also* Organizations
Growth: and challenge to those who prepare leaders, 88; as cornerstone of learning communities, 25; and curriculum, 95, 103; implications for school leadership of, 25; and phases of values consciousness, 45; and principals as developing leaders, 54, 55, 58, 59, 60, 71; and servant leadership, 81. *See also* Groups: development of; Growth cycle; Individual development; Leadership development
Growth cycle, 4, 8, 40–42, 43, 72, 82, 85, 116. *See also* Phases of values consciousness; *stage in cycle*
Grumwald, B. B., 12
Guskey, T. R., 124

Hall, B., 4–5, 6, 31, 38, 40, 41, 43–46, 47, 49, 73, 76–77, 78, 82. *See also* Growth cycle; Phases of values consciousness
Hall, G. E., 113, 122, 127
Haller, E. J., 36, 92, 117, 118
Hannay, L. M., 123
Hare, A., 14
Hawthorne, R. D., 98, 99, 100, 106
Henderson, J. G., 98, 99, 100, 106
Herbert, F., 16
Herrmond, D., 3, 13, 29, 73
Hersey, P., 13
Herzberg, F., 12
Hill, M., 16, 104, 117, 125
Hodgkinson, C., 31, 32, 36, 38
Hole, S., 123
Holland, P., 11
Hooker, R., 3, 125
Hord, S. M., 113, 127
Hunter, M., 110, 111, 115, 120

Independence phase of values consciousness, 82, 85
Individual development, 15, 31, 45, 116; and care, 77, 78; continuum of, 20–24; and curriculum, 96, 98–99, 103; and impact of work about leadership development, 129–31; and leadership modes, 83, 84, 85; and learning communities, 4, 9, 19–24, 25, 119–20, 124, 125; and principals as developing leaders, 56, 71, 73, 107; psychological perspective of, 19–24. *See also* Growth cycle; Phases of values consciousness
Individual growth plans, 105–6
Individualistic values stage, 39, 41
Individualized educational plans, 72–73
Individuals: group applications versus, 119–20
Institutional growth cycle/values consciousness, 40–41, 42, 43, 63, 64, 69, 70, 76, 78, 82, 84–85
Instruction, 10, 14, 73, 100–108, 119, 122, 125
Integrated values stage, 39, 41
Interaction, 4, 21, 25, 39, 100, 101, 108
Interdependence, 76, 130; and curriculum, 98, 99; and individual development, 21, 98; and leadership modes, 82; and learning communities, 4, 21, 25, 39, 122; and

nature of groups, 14, 15, 16, 18–19; and values, 36, 39, 45, 82
Interdependent leadership, 82
Internships, 2, 96, 103
Interpersonal growth cycle/values consciousness, 41, 42, 43, 58, 59, 76, 78, 82, 85
Interstate School Leaders Licensure Consortium (ISLLC), 93, 94–95
Intuition, 23, 28, 29, 30, 45

Johnson, D. W., 14, 15, 17, 99, 100, 102, 103, 108, 131
Johnson, R. T., 14, 15, 17, 99, 100, 102, 103, 108, 131
Journals, 2–3, 22, 46, 79; and cohort studies, 15–16; and curriculum, 103, 107–8; and impact of work about leadership development, 129, 131; and principals as developing leaders, 48, 49, 50, 56, 60; and values, 34–35, 36, 49
Justice: ethic of, 36, 86

Kasten, K., 11, 16
Kempner, K., 117
Kerrins, J. A., 104
King, P., 113
Kitchener, K., 112
Knowledge/knowledge acquisition, 1, 78, 84; and challenge to those who prepare leaders, 89–90; creation of, 30; and curriculum, 7, 92–93, 109; and impact of work about leadership development, 129, 130, 131, 135–36, 137; and individual development, 21, 23; and learning communities, 9, 10, 25, 30, 39, 40; and learning transfer, 113; shared, 30, 36, 45, 71, 87, 89–90, 131, 137; and transformational leadership, 86, 87; and values, 4, 36, 40, 44, 45
Knowles, M., 89, 97
Kohlberg, L., 36, 38
Kolb, David, 105, 113, 114
Kottkamp, R., 48
Kouzes, J. M., 32, 33, 48, 72, 80, 99, 105
Krathwohl, D., 34, 37, 38, 78, 79
Krueger, J., 117
Kultgen, J., 36

Leaders/leadership: continuum of, 6–7; definition of, 81, 85; functions of, 31; implications of learning communities for, 25–30; and leader as follower, 85; modes of, 6–7, 82–85; as moral act, 75; nature of, 31–34; pathways of development of, 38–40; and power, 83; as role models, 52; role of, 51, 52, 58, 60, 83, 85; and values, 31–47, 72, 82. *See also* Leadership development/leadership development programs; *specific mode*

Leadership development/leadership development programs: aims of, 37, 46, 92, 109; benefits of, 117–18; challenge of, 88–90, 126; criticisms of, 72, 84, 92–93; historical, 5; and impact on subsequent performance of graduates, 117–18; and leadership modes, 7, 84, 85; and learning communities, 4, 123; learning transfer in, 116–25; legacy of, 126; meaning of, 38; overview about, 1, 2; standards for, 93–96; students' experience in, 50; and transformational leadership, 88; and values, 31–47

Learners/learning: change and reflection of, 113–14; constructivist approach to, 2, 96, 97–98, 101, 103; cycle of, 113–14; double-loop, 86; experiential, 7, 33, 37, 89–90, 104, 113; and impact of work about leadership development, 129; integrated approach to, 50; as journey, 129–30; and learning communities, 1, 118, 123–24; and learning transfer, 112, 113–14, 115; as lifelong/continual process, 52, 59, 86–87, 95; and principals as developing leaders, 52, 53, 56, 59, 61, 66–67; problem-based, 2, 103, 107, 129; team, 27, 29, 86; and transformational leadership, 86–87; and values, 45; views about, 25–26. *See also* Personal Mastery

Learning communities: beliefs and assumptions about, 10–11; benefits of, 7, 131; challenges concerning, 12, 88, 118–22; characteristics of, 27–30, 100, 119–20, 126, 127; commonalities among, 2; conceptualization of, 4, 13–14; functions/importance of, 9, 10–12; future investigations about, 126–28; impact of, 127; and impact of work about leadership development, 131–37; implications for school leadership of, 25–30; and internal and external forces, 121–22, 127; legacy of, 7, 110–28; model for, 5, 8, 24–25, 26, 39–41, 77, 116, 131–37; need for, 10–12; overview of, 1–8, 9–10, 126–28; power of, 10; psychological perspective of, 19–24; as reflective communities, 104; sociological perspectives of, 14–15, 16–19; spontaneous evolution of, 1; strategies for encouraging, 122–25; and transfer, 116–25; university-based, 3; and values, 36, 37, 39–40, 42, 45. *See also* Cohorts; *specific topic*

Learning transfer: concept of, 111–12; and curriculum, 104, 109; definition of, 110; dilemmas for, 119; factors affecting, 112–16; final thoughts about, 125–26; follow-up on, 123; framework for, 122–23; goal/importance of, 7, 110, 111–12; impact of, 124–25; and impact of work about leadership development, 130; and individual versus group application, 119–20; lack of empirical evidence supporting successful, 112; in leadership development programs, 116–18; and learning communities, 4, 7, 10, 110–28; responsibility for, 122–23; timing of, 122–23; to workplace, 116–25

Lee, A. Y., 119
Leithwood, K., 118, 125
Levine, S., 32, 97
Levinson, D., 6, 25, 27, 32, 136
Lightfoot, S., 6
Little, J., 11, 120
Loeser, L., 14
Loevinger, J., 38–41

McBrien, J. L., 97
McClellan, D., 12
McEntee, G. H., 123
McGrath, J., 14
McLaughlin, M. W., 115, 120, 121, 127
McNeil, J., 99, 100, 104
Mahony, G., 123
Management, 6–7, 85
Marini, A., 112
Marshall, C., 11
Maslach, C., 11, 77
Maslow, A., 12
May, L., 34
Meisgeier, C., 3, 13, 29, 73
Melaville, A. I., 123

Mental models, 27, 28, 86, 87
Merriam, S. B., 97, 100, 101, 103
Miller, R., 97
Milstein, M. M., 100, 102, 105, 109, 117
Mintzberg, H., 28
Morgan, G., 5, 6, 42, 43–46, 47, 49, 82, 83
Murphy, J., 36, 37, 84, 92, 96, 100, 101, 126
Muse, I. D., 97, 100, 101, 102, 103, 104, 105, 118
Muth, R., 127
Mystical growth cycle/values, 41, 42, 43, 76, 77, 78, 82

National Association of Elementary Principals, 93
National Center for Education Statistics, 11
National Commission for the Principalship, 92
National Policy Board for Educational Administration (NPBEA), 93, 95
NCATE, 93, 94
Needs/needs theory, 12–13, 42, 44, 76, 88–89
New order phase of values consciousness, 82
Noddings, Nel, 37, 75
Norman, Brad, 56–60
Norris, Cynthia J., 2–3, 9, 13, 14, 15, 20, 28, 29, 32, 33, 49, 73, 75, 85, 86, 97, 99, 102, 110, 117, 125, 126, 130, 137
Norton, M. S., 125

Organizational metaphors: brain, 5, 43, 45, 46, 55; and leadership mode, 7; machine, 5, 43, 44, 45, 63, 64, 69, 70, 83; organism, 5, 43, 44, 45, 58, 59, 63, 64, 70, 71; and phases of values consciousness, 5, 42, 43–46; and principals as developing leaders, 47, 49, 55, 58, 59, 63, 64, 69, 70, 71–72
Organizational theory, 73
Organizations: and development of learning communities, 119; and learning transfer, 115–16; and nature of leadership, 32; preservation of, 32; and values, 32. See also Groups
Ottoson, J. M., 111

Parents/families, 11, 66, 80, 94
Parsons, T., 31

Partnerships, 119, 121–22, 123, 125
Patterson High School (Colorado), 65–71
Peck, S., 107
Pennington, N., 119
Performance skills, 1, 7, 9, 10, 40
Personal dream, 4, 78, 125; and curriculum, 100, 104; functions/importance of, 32, 34; and impact of work about leadership development, 130, 136–37; and individual development, 21, 24; and learning communities, 25, 27, 28, 39, 40, 118; and nature of leadership, 32, 34; and principals as developing leaders, 5, 51, 56, 58, 61, 62; and values, 32, 34
Personal growth. See Individual development
Personal mastery, 27–28, 86–87
Peterson, K. D., 121
Phases of values consciousness (Hall), 4–5, 7, 38, 40, 85, 89; and care, 76–77, 78; and first phase, 42, 43, 44, 76, 78; and fourth phase, 42, 43, 45, 55, 76, 78; and leadership modes, 7, 82; and Loevinger's values theory, 38, 39; and organizational metaphors, 5, 42; organizational metaphors compared with, 43–46; and principals as developing leaders, 47, 54, 55, 58, 63, 64, 69, 70, 72; and second phase, 42, 43, 44–45, 63, 64, 69, 70, 76, 78; and third phase, 42, 43, 45, 58, 76, 78; and transformational leadership, 5, 87
Piaget, J., 97
Platforms, 13, 46, 106, 129; functions of, 48–49, 106; integration of leadership development programs and, 73; points to consider when using, 72–73; and principals as developing leaders, 5, 48–49, 50, 51, 52, 60, 65, 67, 69, 71, 72
Plato, 111
Portfolios, 46, 60, 103, 106–7, 129
Portraitures, 5, 46–47, 49–50. See also Crawford, Bob; Norman, Brad; Smithfield, Amy; Williams, Ross
Posner, B. Z., 32, 33, 48, 72, 80, 99, 105
Power, 10, 44, 45, 83, 86
Primal growth cycle, 40, 41, 42, 43, 76, 78, 82
Principals: as developing leaders, 48–74; as instructional leaders, 85; and leadership modes, 85; loneliness of, 62; and

phases of values consciousness, 45; role of, 25, 51. *See also* Crawford, Bob; Norman, Brad; Smithfield, Amy; Williams, Ross

Problem finding/solving, 13, 32, 86, 89, 119, 129; and curriculum, 99, 103; and nature of groups, 14, 18–19; and principals as developing leaders, 50, 68, 73; sequestered, 119

Problem-based learning activities, 2, 103, 107, 129

Problem-based learning groups. *See* Learning communities

Professional organizations, 95, 96

Professors: assessment of, 96; caring by, 88; challenge to, 88–90; and curriculum, 95, 96, 97–98, 100–102, 103, 104–5, 108; and empowerment, 13; and leadership modes, 84; and learning communities, 10, 120; and learning transfer, 117–18; and nature of groups, 14, 17–18; and principals as developing leaders, 50, 51; as role models, 95; role of, 10, 14, 96, 100–102; student relationship with, 97–98, 101–2; and transformational leadership, 88

Prophetic growth cycle, 82

Purpose: and Loevinger's values theory, 39; and model for learning communities, 4, 21, 25, 39

"Purposing," 36

Rath, Louis E., 12

Razik, R., 31

Reflection, 33, 79, 86–87, 118; and curriculum, 99, 100, 102, 104, 107; and impact of work about leadership development, 129, 130, 131–37; and learning communities, 2, 7, 28, 104, 123–24; and learning transfer, 113–14; and principals as developing leaders, 48, 50, 60, 61, 65, 72, 73; stages/levels of, 113; and values, 33, 39, 45

Reflective writings. *See* Journals

Relationships, 13–14, 86, 117–18, 125; and curriculum, 97–98, 101–2, 104; faculty-student, 97–98, 101–2; and principals as developing leaders, 62, 66–67, 68, 69; and values, 39, 42, 45. *See also* Care; Connections; Friendship; Teamwork

Responsibility, 103, 122–23; and care, 76, 77, 79; and leadership modes, 83, 85; and principals as developing leaders, 60, 61, 67, 71; of transformational leadership, 85–87; and values, 35, 46

Rewards, 8, 52, 61, 83, 136

Reynolds, K., 16

Rights/world order phase of values consciousness, 82

Rogers, E. M., 99, 115, 119–20, 127

Role models, 52, 53, 56, 66, 95

San Diego State University, 2

San Diego Unified School District, 94

Sandoval, G., 11

Schein, E. H., 121

Schmidt, W., 13

Schnur, S. I., 117

Schön, D. A., 104, 106, 114

Schwartz, D. L., 110, 112, 114, 116, 119

Security, 84, 126; and care, 76, 78; and growth cycles, 4, 40; and impact of work about leadership development, 130, 132–33; and individual development, 20–22; and learning communities, 25, 39–40; and values, 38, 39–40, 44, 82, 83–84

Self-actualization, 12, 13, 27, 41, 45, 58, 60, 98

Self-awareness/understanding, 24, 76; and curriculum, 99, 104; and learning communities, 10, 28; and principals as developing leaders, 50, 60, 67, 72–73; and values, 31–32, 38, 39, 46

Self-competence phase of values consciousness, 82

Self-protective values stage, 38, 39, 41

Self-renewal, 25, 45, 86, 87

Self-worth phase of values consciousness, 82

Senge, P. M., 13, 15, 25, 27, 28, 29, 30, 32, 33, 36, 46, 86, 87

Sergiovanni, T., 6, 36, 48–49, 73, 80–81, 83, 84, 85, 106

"Servant leader," 6, 75, 79, 80–82

Shaw, M., 11, 15

Short, P. M., 104

Skills/means, 42, 43, 77, 129. *See also* Performance skills

Smith, K. A., 100, 108

Smith, L., 122

Smithfield, Amy, 51–56
Snowy Range Cohort, 56
Sparks, D., 124
Sparks-Langer, G. M., 113
Spindler, G., 11
Spindler, L., 11
Standards, 7, 93–96, 103, 108, 109
Starratt, R., 36, 48–49, 73, 104, 106, 118, 119
Sternberg, R. J., 112, 115, 120
Strain, J. M., 11
Strike, K., 36
Structure, 34, 39, 44, 84, 85, 120, 126
Students, 50, 80, 103; and curriculum, 97–98; and empowerment, 12–13; faculty relationship with, 97–98, 101–2; and principals as developing leaders, 53, 57, 62, 66–67, 68, 70, 71; role of, 49
Study groups, 13, 14
Support, 13, 33, 78, 87, 115; and curriculum, 100, 105, 108; and group development, 17, 100; and impact of work about leadership development, 130, 131–32, 138; and individual development, 20, 21, 22; and learning communities, 25, 39–40, 123; and principals as developing leaders, 67, 73; and values, 4, 33, 39–40
Survival/security phase of values consciousness, 82, 83–84
Swanson, A., 31
Systems thinking, 27, 29–30

Tannenbaum, R., 13
Tasks, 13–14, 45, 83, 112, 114–15
Teachers, 11, 80, 120–21; as facilitators, 66; and principals as developing leaders, 53–54, 57–58, 61–63, 65, 67–69, 70, 71–72, 118; role of, 49, 67, 71. *See also* Professors
Teams: as characteristic of learning communities, 27, 29; and curriculum, 105; and learning, 27, 29, 86; and principals as developing leaders, 58, 61, 63, 65, 66, 67, 68, 69, 70, 71; and transformational leadership, 86. *See also* Learning communities
Texas Association of Secondary School Principals, 51
Theory in use, 5, 46, 86, 89; and nature of leadership, 32–33; and principals as de-

veloping leaders, 48, 49–50, 53–54, 55, 56, 58, 59, 60, 62–63, 65, 67–69, 71–72
Thinking, 12, 13, 27, 28, 29–30, 45, 88–90
Thompson, H., 31, 38, 40
Thorndike, E., 112
Timing, 62, 122–23
Tracom Corporation, 105
Transactional leadership, 6–7, 82, 83–84
Transactional-transformational leadership, 7, 82, 84–85
Transformational leadership, 1, 18, 26, 74, 118, 137–38; and care, 75–79; characteristics of, 7, 82, 85–86; conceptualization and development of, 75–90, 126; and curriculum, 91, 96; ethical responsibilities of, 85–87; and impact of work about leadership development, 137–38; and leadership modes, 6, 7, 82–83; and learning communities, 7, 10, 25; and management, 6, 85; need for, 87–88; and servant leadership, 80–82; and values, 5, 34, 37, 40, 45, 46
Triangle: as learning community model, 20, 24, 25, 26, 116
Trubowitz, S., 122
Trueba, H., 11
Trust, 33, 118, 132; and curriculum, 94, 104–5; and individual development, 20, 22, 23; and learning communities, 29, 30, 121, 122; and principals as developing leaders, 48, 62, 63, 67, 73
Tucker, M. C., 103
Twale, D. J., 104

Ubben, G., 33
Universities: cross-collaboration among, 4; and curriculum, 91, 96; learning communities based in, 3; and need for learning communities, 12; school partnerships with, 119, 122. *See also specific institution*
University of Houston, 2, 3, 15, 50–51, 88. *See also* Smithfield, Amy
University of Indiana, 2
University of North Colorado, 50–51. *See also* Crawford, Bob
University of Northern Colorado, 2, 15, 50, 65
University of Tennessee, 2
University of Wyoming, 2, 15, 50–51, 56. *See also* Norman, Brad

Valley League of Schools (California), 65
Values: and aims of leadership development programs, 46; and care, 76–77, 78;
and challenge to those who prepare leaders, 88–90; characterizing, 35–36, 37; clarification of, 2, 13, 28, 29, 32, 33, 46, 47,
48, 72, 74, 89; and credibility, 32–33; and
curriculum, 104–5; development of, 34–
36, 40–41, 46; embodiment of, 32; and
ethics, 36–38; impact of, 33; and individual development, 24; internalizing/orga-
nizing, 35, 37; and leadership development, 31–47; leadership as extension of
individual, 72; and learning communities, 2, 3, 9, 10, 27, 28, 29, 31–47, 118;
Loevinger's stage theory of, 38–41; and
nature of leadership, 31–34; and organizations, 32; and portraitures, 46, 47; and
principals as developing leaders, 48, 71,
72, 73–74; shared, 27, 29, 36, 104–5; theory of, 12, 13; and transformational leadership, 34, 86–87; and values development, 33, 36; valuing, 33, 35, 37. *See also*
Espoused theory; Growth cycle; Phases
of values consciousness
Vince, R., 113, 114

Vineyard Middle School (California),
61–65
Vision, 13, 32, 87, 89; and curriculum, 94,
95, 100; and learning communities, 28,
29, 118; platforms as basis for developing, 73; and principals as developing
leaders, 54, 57, 60, 61, 62, 63, 67, 69, 71,
73. *See also* Personal dream
Vygotsky, L. S., 97

Wasserman, S., 12, 88
Weise, K., 3, 11, 125
Whitaker, K. S., 123
White, E. M., 115
Williams, Ross, 60–65
Wilson, P., 98
Wingspread Group in Higher Eduction, 92
Workplace: differences between cohorts
and, 120–21; transfer to, 109, 110–28

Yerkes, D., 3, 14, 15, 20, 49, 73, 99, 100,
101, 102, 110, 117, 125, 126, 129, 130, 137

Zaleznik, A., 83
Zander, A., 15

About the Authors

Bruce G. Barnett is a professor and Director of the Division of Educational Leadership and Policy Studies at the University of Northern Colorado. An often-cited writer with much experience in leadership development, he has stayed at his university since the beginning of our work together, notwithstanding a sabbatical to work with principals in Australia.

Margaret (Peg) R. Basom was an associate professor and later department chair at the University of Wyoming as we journeyed together. A respected educational leader in her state and region, she subsequently moved to San Diego State University where she is coordinating the preliminary credential program and directing an international program for master's students.

Cynthia J. Norris, former associate professor at the University of Houston, who said we should reach for our own personal dreams and write a book about our work, has relocated to her home state and the University of Tennessee. Her guidance, leadership, and passion for this topic have inspired us all.

Diane M. Yerkes, a professor at California State University, Fresno, brought years of experience in leadership development for principals to the group. She also has moved to San Diego State University, perhaps evidence of the power of the community, as she and Peg now work together. She leads the professional credential program and is coordinating a new facilitated distance learning program.